IN THE SHADOW

by | ISAAC S. DENNIS

IN THE SHADOW
by ISAAC S. DENNIS

Printed in the United States of America

ISBN 1-890430-31-5
Copyright © 2006 by Isaac S. Dennis

Isaac S. Dennis
Angom World Ministries
C/O Interlink Christian Network
PO Box 380 292
Brooklyn NY 11238, USA
www.dennisintheshadow.com
info@dennisintheshadow.com

Published By:
Triumph Publishing
P. O. Box 690158
Bronx, New York, 10469
www.triumphpublishing.net

DEDICATION

This book is dedicated to the Almighty God.

To all who played a major part in helping me live
through the experiences in this book.

To every member of my ministry worldwide.

And to all those who have worked hard to see
the birth of "In The Shadow."

TABLE OF CONTENTS

Author's Note

This book is based on a true story of a young man who gave up his own dreams to accomplish a special mission for God.

All scripture passages quoted or referenced in this work have been taken from the Authorized King James Version of the Bible.

FOREWORD

What Isaac Dennis has chronicled in his book, In the Shadow, are extraordinary happenings in the life of an individual. These events show many things that are occurring inside of human experiences that many people never have an opportunity to see or experience in their lifetime. The very fact that he is a living witness to this divine encounter and experience as a human being is extraordinary to say the least.

The book chronicles the fact that no matter where you are born in this world, the omnipotent, ever-present power of God is there and that through divine providence and predetermination, God orchestrates the lives of certain individuals in a special way. We see that when one experiences the touch of God in their lives, no matter how daunting the circumstances surrounding that person, they can overcome and accomplish impossible things!

Isaac Dennis' pure innocent faith led him to follow the light not only into the spiritual darkness of an uncertain future but through the literal darkness of physical Africa. Through the occultism, idolatrous and demonic powers so prevalent in Africa, he took his physical journey from Nigeria to the Ivory Coast where "The light" was leading him. The long nights on the road as he trekked his way to that New Land and Place of his Destiny was a real physical play out of what was really and truly happening in his spiritual world as a new babe in Christ.

The incredible experience he had on the road would have caused many to turn back but he kept going, determined to get to the destination "The Light" had spoken of. This strange person which indeed was "The Angel of the Lord" met and communicated with him and guided him out of very dangerous situations. The situations that could have aborted his mission and possibly have taken his life, confirm the truth of the light leading him. A light that has brought him to where he is today and is a testimony of profound intrigue that has all the elements of mystery, supernatural intrigue, drama and action of biblical proportions!

This book is going to be one of the most intriguing documents of our time for several reasons, first, because of the nature of the experiences involved and second is that the person to whom these things happened is alive to tell the story. The effects of these experiences are still evolving. We have yet to see unfold before our eyes the divine purpose providence had in orchestrating this experience in Africa and now in America, with one of His chosen vessels.

In The Shadow" is not an ordinary book. It is unique and different in many respects in that it tells the story more than it preaches. The story speaks for itself. It will be a great source of inspiration, revelation, insight and encouragement for everyone looking for answers to life's mysteries, hope and help from higher sources and faith to believe that there is a God at work in human affairs. It tells us that the God of the Bible who visited His people in visions and revelations and angels is still doing so today.

I highly recommend this book to believers in Christ, to scholars, teachers, scientists, atheists and the other entire religious groups who are sincerely reaching and trying to find the true and living God. This is a living story of a living human being with a living experience with the living God, who is yet living today to tell it. May God thrill your soul as you read this living account.

Bishop W. R. Portee
Southside Christian Palace
Los Angeles, California

INTRODUCTION

It is not often that you read a book so captivating you cannot put it down. In the Shadow fits well into this category. Isaac Dennis takes the reader through his own journey from his native country of Nigeria to Sierra Leone and how God took him from a series of hopeless situations to a place of rest, victory and demonstration of His power. His love and adamant resolution to bring light to a people who sit in darkness is a wonder to behold. For the sake of the Gospel, Isaac left his homeland, Nigeria, to traverse many countries to a land he had never been before. The miracles that follow each other in dire situations cannot but invoke a sense of awe and wonder at the amazing power of God to solve insurmountable situations. The reader sits on the edge of their seat as he/she reads the account of the events that led the author to where he is today. The accounts are vivid, captivating and true.

It is a book of pain and joy, pain because of the terrible situations the Sierra Leones have gone through, the darkness that covered them and their city, the cruelty and the lawlessness of the rebels and its grave consequences on their fellow citizens. Yet, joy and victory emerge as the power of God brought salvation, healing, deliverance to hopeless situations through his instrument, Isaac Dennis, as he boldly proclaimed the Gospel of Jesus Christ.

This book, without doubt, will have a far reaching impact not just only on fulfilling one's purpose as is dramatically presented here in the life of Isaac Dennis, but will help the believer to rethink their love for Christ and how much they are willing to suffer for Him.

I pray that as this book goes forth, it will bring healing to the sick, light to those who sit in darkness, peace to the troubled heart, encouragement to the despondent, faith to the hopeless and burning fire to all believers to go forth with the Gospel of Jesus Christ which is the power of God for salvation. I recommend this book.

Dr. Tai Ikomi
Triumph Christian Ministries,
Bronx, NY

CHAPTER ONE
BURNING WITH A VISION

CHAPTER ONE
Burning With a Vision

"I am Jesus Christ. I have called you and chosen you.
I have ordained you."

I always knew my life was destined for greatness. My dream of becoming a great movie star was simply unshakable, although I had no idea how it would happen. My plan was to practice things I saw on the screen, which I did constantly so I would be ready when the big break came. Not only was I certain of this destiny for myself, I received encouragement and support from my family to follow my dreams. In my early childhood in Benin City, Nigeria, my father instilled a solid belief in my ability to achieve great goals in life. My sights stayed high as a teenager living with my mother in the small town of Sabo in Edo State. I always believed I would succeed.

We were not wealthy, but we had a comfortable family life, even though we did not always have electricity. We lived in a small town where electricity was not always available. The fifth child of nine children, I lived with two sisters, two younger brothers, and my mother, while my older sister and three brothers had already established themselves in other cities.

My mother was a preacher in a local group called the Adam Preaching Society, but religious matters held no interest for me. I never wanted to be a religious man. My family cared for me and taught me Christian principles, we believed in the existence of God, but no matter how often they encouraged me to attend church, they could not convince me to go. I knew what I wanted to do, and my plans to attend acting school and become a star were resolute.

In 1986, at the age of 18, I learned that God had His own plan for my life. My faith in God would be both shaken and strengthened by one single life-changing event.

One evening after our usual family dinner, we said goodnight. My mother offered her well-worn admonition to turn my lantern down low, but I didn't. I always made sure that my light was burned brightly when I went to bed. It was close to midnight when sleep began to overtake me, but suddenly I felt something different in my bedroom. My eyelids opened to reveal the lantern very dimly lit, eclipsed by a different, much brighter light filling the room from an unknown source. I could not lift myself from the bed. As my head rested on my pillow, I felt supremely confident with my eyes fixed on the light. There was no thought of getting up to see what was happening, just self-assurance that the light was the only thing I needed. Suddenly, the light was replaced by nothingness. My eyes closed, and when I opened them I was suspended in the air, no longer in my room.

A cloud filled my vision, and then broke to reveal a bright light shining directly on me, its rays illuminating my head and face. As I looked at the light, a Hand come out of the light and rested on my head. I cannot describe in any human language how glorious the Hand was, how exquisitely beautiful, how awesome It looked, and splendid It felt to see It and have It near me. I believe It was the Glory of God Himself. Then a Voice began to pray for me.

The Voice spoke to me, "I am Jesus Christ. I have called you and chosen you. I have ordained you. I release My Anointing upon your life to go into the world and preach the Gospel."

I basked in complete stillness and peace. I felt the joy and warmth of the Voice and had no other thought but to allow the Words to fill my being.

A short time later, the Hand withdrew into the cloud.

"Let me look through the hole where that light is piercing through. Maybe I will see heaven!"

But as the Hand pulled back into the cloud, the hole closed and the cloud covered the opening.

I cried out, "Oh, Lord, why don't You want me to see heaven?"

The Voice said, "Isaac, you will see Heaven, but it is not time for you. Look forward."

In front of me were words written in the cloud, white letters on a beautiful blue background: "Jesus Christ is coming back very soon."

I said to the Lord, "I see something written there that Jesus Christ is coming back very soon."

The Lord told me to look down. "What do you see?" the Voice asked.

"I see a multitude of people as far as my eyes can see without ending."

The Lord said, "I have called you to go into the world and preach to the people that I, Jesus Christ, am coming back very soon."

It was a moment of contentment and resolve that would affect every waking breath, every step, every word, thought and deed for the rest of my life. The Lord had called me and chosen me to do His work.

After this encounter, I found myself back in my own bed. My lantern had resumed its original brightness, and my room was in its normal state. What had happened to me? I felt terrified and overpowered with fear. Wide awake, agitated and confused, I knew sleep would be impossibly. I got out of bed and went down the hall.

My mother awoke to my knock and opened her bedroom door. Her bewilderment turned to concern.

"Isaac, what is wrong with you?" she asked.

"Mama, I cannot sleep in my room any more."

Mama was not one to coddle her children, especially a tall young man of eighteen.

"No, go back and sleep in your room."

"I cannot go in that room."

I dragged a mattress to the floor of my mother's room so I could stay close to her, hoping to quell the anxiety in my heart, but even then I tossed and turned and could not sleep for the rest of the night.

In the morning, my mother called me. "Isaac, what happened to you last night?"

I explained. She listened intently, then looked me straight in the eyes and said the words I will never forget, "God is calling you."

Immediately she began to pray for me. When she finished, she looked up. "This is God that is calling you. He has chosen you as His servant."

"What can I do now?"

"Go to church."

Simple advice, but I was not satisfied. I went to the Church of God mission and explained to the pastor, his name was Pastor Udo, what had happened. He said that this was the call of God and that I should pray, seeking the Lord and asking God in what area He was calling me.

"In what area?"

The pastor explained there were different callings in the five-fold ministry: Apostle, Prophet, Evangelist, Pastor, Teacher.

> *And he gave some, apostles; and some, prophets; and some, evangelists; and some, pastors and teachers (Ephesians 4:11).*

That evening I prayed. "God, are You the One calling me? If you are the One, I want You to show me again what You want me to do."

God answered me immediately. I saw a vision of thousands of people gathered around me on a stage. In the vision, I preached to the multitude and then prayed for them. I saw a crippled man healed and able to walk right on the stage. People jubilated and rejoiced at the miracle.

In the morning when I awoke, I thought about everything that had been revealed to me. The vision played again in my mind, but it was a difficult thing. I didn't know what to do or how to handle myself. I went back to Pastor Udo and told him of my experience. I had never seen anything like it before. I had never been to a crusade, or seen a crippled man healed. He told me he believed that God had called me into the ministry of an evangelist.

He asked me to kneel down and he prayed for me. From that time I started going to church, studying the scriptures and the gospel. This was a profound change in me. I would lay down my dreams and embark on a mission to save others, but not everyone would understand.

One evening, my family discussed ways to help me further my career as a movie star. They planned to put me into acting school, because this was something that had always burned so brightly in me. When my sponsorship was ready, my older brother came to take me to acting school.

"No, Brother, I have changed my mind. I am not going to acting school any more. I want to go to the Bible College. God has called me and that is what I want to do."

My brother was not happy about my decision; it was a disappointment to him and to the rest of my family. They all thought I was crazy, that something was wrong with me. The chance to attend acting school had been my life-long dream, and I, too felt sorry to give it up. But I knew I needed to do what God asked me to do. He was more important than my career, my personal aspirations, or what other people thought.

Each night I talked with God and I always received an answer immediately.

So that same year, I went to Bible College, devoted myself to my studies, and graduated in two years.

After graduation in 1989, I went to live with my older brother and was sure there would be a job waiting for me. With so many churches around, I thought certainly everything would go smoothly. After all, God had called me. I was serving a big God who could do anything and everything, and I would start out on the top of the world. According to the vision I had seen, I was going to preach to multitudes of people very soon. I would get everything I asked for, everything in my reach all at once. I aimed high. I would climb to the pinnacle.

However, there is a time to have a vision and a time for it to come to pass. The first shock came during my visit to a church. I told them I had been called by God to be an evangelist. The pastor looked at me very strangely and treated me as if I were nobody.

"We don't just take somebody to work in the church as an evangelist or whatever you call yourself," he said. He rudely pushed me in the corner and told me to sit over there and be part of the Bible class.

I went from church to church introducing myself, hoping to find a place to fulfill my destiny, but my experiences heaped one disappointment after another on my head. Upset and frustrated, I prayed, "God, lead me where you want me to go."

The administrator of a local church asked me to submit a letter of application along with my curriculum vitae. He said there was a job for me in the church serving as an evangelist. When I heard that I was very excited. I knew finally this was the moment my vision would come to pass. The required documents were submitted and I waited for some weeks before receiving a reply. It finally arrived and I tore open the mail eagerly, searching for the words that would answer my prayers.

They regretted they could not employ me in any position in their ministry and hoped I would make it somewhere else. As I laid aside the letter, I felt frustrated, and confused.

I went back to the administrator to ask why they had rejected me. My application was in order, but they felt my young age made me too immature to enter the ministry. I was twenty-one years old. The administrator asked if I was sure I wanted to embark on a career as a minister.

"Yes, because I know God has called me for this purpose. I desire nothing else. It is as a fire shut up in my bones."

In spite of my conviction, he asked me to consider looking for another job. The church that I had hoped would be a haven, in which my ministry would grow and expand, had left me in an alley with nowhere to turn. I was fast running out of options.

For months I had nothing to do. No church in the city would accept me. I decided if nobody would give me a job, I would create one for myself. But I didn't know how to go about it. Confused, bombarded with rejections from family, friends, and pastors, I began to doubt my ability to make it in the ministry.

> *I am the LORD, your Holy One, the creator of Israel, your King. Thus saith the LORD, which maketh a way in the sea, and a path in the mighty waters (Isaiah 43:15-16).*

I had no other choice but to trust In God. He had called me; He would make a way for me. I began leaving the city, traveling around Nigeria looking for a job. Sometimes a journey took six hours and sometimes one or two days. All my efforts were fruitless. I went into villages to preach and organize outreach meetings. Nothing was working.

My older brother called me and said that being an evangelist was messing up my life. He said if I wanted to continue, I would have to find somewhere else to live. I returned to his house, moved my things outside and sat there for hours. I had nowhere to go; I was homeless.

I walked almost four hours that night. I remembered one of my old friends from Bible College and went to look for him, to ask for a place to lay my head. Fortunately, I found him at home and explained my condition. He had no room, so I slept outside on the balcony for a couple of days until his mother arranged a place for me to sleep in an inside passageway of the house.

Sometimes I would visit friends in other towns for one or two days in order to have a good place to sleep. Moving from place to place, I prayed for God's direction and guidance to lead me to the work He had called me to do. The scripture gave me courage: if you commit your ways unto the Lord, He will guide and direct your path. This knowledge was the anchor of my faith during this trying time.

My condition had become terrible. Memories of the loving family who had cared for me haunted my thoughts. Now,

honoring the call of God had put me out of my home, rejected and driven away from the house where I once enjoyed
acceptance and love.

"Where can I go?" became my constant prayer. "God, lead
me. Open doors for me." As I prayed, my heart twisted in
anguish and tears poured down my face. I closed my eyes and
waited expectantly for the Lord to speak to my distraught soul.

CHAPTER TWO
PURPOSE WITHOUT ACTION

CHAPTER TWO
Purpose Without Action

It was up to me to discover God's plan for my life. I became convinced during this time that if my own plans did not go in the direction I expected, it was because God had other plans for me. I pinned all my hope and faith on God, and continued to depend on Him.

When I had no food, I decided God wanted me to fast.

When I saw people walking in the streets talking to themselves, I no longer wondered why they were troubled. I began to understand through firsthand experience the tremendous stress of not knowing what to do, where to go, or who to turn to for help. The overwhelming worry of daily survival weighed heavily on my nerves. As I observed others in similarly precarious positions, I saw myself in them. It was as if they were dramatizing my own doubts. Why would God allow these hardships if He had truly called me to preach His word.

God was indeed tempering me in the fire of adversity, strengthening me to be able to fulfill a great destiny. The life of Apostle Paul offers an example of challenges in a missionary's experience. Although he had been called to preach after his Damascus experience, and even with the prayers of the Church behind him, Paul still went through life-threatening situations. And yet, in a spirit of encouragement to the believers going through difficult times, he wrote:

> *If we suffer, we shall also reign with [him]:*
> *if we deny [him], he also will deny us*
> *(2 Timothy 2:12).*

One day as I prayed, the Lord opened my eyes to a map of West Africa. I saw myself stepping from one country to another on the map until I stood on one country. The name written on it was "Sierra Leone." I didn't know where Sierra Leone was and I had to look in the atlas to find it. I called a friend and told him I had seen myself walking into West Africa and stopping in Sierra Leone. I showed him the map. This was where God had called me to preach. That day, I started planning my journey to Freetown, Sierra Leone, through the West Coast of Africa.

I had no contacts in Sierra Leone no means of communication, and no knowledge of what lay before me. Traveling to Sierra Leone would be difficult, because I could not afford airfare and there was no bus going there. The journey by road would cost five thousand naira, about fifty dollars. There was no internet or helpful website to guide me, but I simply believed this was where the Lord was taking me and He would make a way for me to get there.

I would preach to anyone who would listen. With no one supporting me, I had to take a step of faith. Having a great purpose in life without taking a step towards it leads to stag-nation. I could not allow fear to stop me from acting.

> *Even so faith, if it hath not works, is dead,*
> *being alone (James 2:17).*

"Take a step that no one can take for you."

The Lord would reward me for putting my faith into action.

> *But without faith [it is] impossible to please*
> *[him]: for he that cometh to God must believe*
> *that he is, and [that] he is a rewarder of them*
> *that diligently seek him (Hebrews 11:6).*

My dilemma was grim: cancel the trip, stay in my present state of destitution, or go ahead into the unknown without enough money to get to my destination. I didn't know what to do. I was so frustrated. Nobody believed that I could make it, because the possibility for success was too remote. "Isaac, God didn't call you to do this. Why don't you give up and do something else with your life?"

There was no going back, no standing still, and only one way to succeed: by moving forward. My life was a gift for the Lord's mission.

CHAPTER THREE
A JOURNEY IN THE SHADOW

CHAPTER THREE
A Journey in the Shadow

With five hundred naira, five dollars, I decided to start my journey from Nigeria to Sierra Leone. Because I needed to cross many different countries before I reached Freetown, my prayer was, "God, I put this journey before You; open the door for me and grant me favor on the way." One scripture in particular spoke to me:

> *And he said unto them, Go ye into all the world, and preach the gospel to every creature. He that believeth and is baptized shall be saved; but he that believeth not shall be damned. And these signs shall follow them that believe; In my name shall they cast out devils; they shall speak with new tongues; They shall take up serpents; and if they drink any deadly thing, it shall not hurt them; they shall lay hands on the sick, and they shall recover (Mark 16:15-18).*

I also read about how, when the disciples went forth to preach, the Lord worked with them in signs and wonders. I read Jesus' commandment to His disciples:

> *Therefore said he unto them, The harvest truly is great, but the labourers are few: pray ye therefore the Lord of the harvest, that he would send forth labourers into his harvest. Go your ways: behold, I send you forth as lambs among wolves. Carry neither purse, nor scrip, nor shoes: and salute no man by the way (Luke 10:2-4).*

All I could take with me were a few clothes. I had to believe that God would make a way for me at every point of my journey, making it truly a journey of faith and experience. What a great learning opportunity for a young man! In time, I would come to understand what it takes to arrive at one's destiny.

I left Benin City and arrived in Lagos, where I hired a taxi to drive me to the Togo / Ghana border. That was as far as my five hundred naira could take me. I slept that night on the beach. Without any money, I wandered in the streets and was looking for the next action plan to take. How would I get to Kumasi, then to Abidjan? Suddenly, it struck me that I was carrying something of value: my clothes. I brought out one of my nice suits and sold it for enough money to take me as far as Kumasi in Ghana, and then I took another bus to the border of Côte d'Ivoire. Again, I slept with nothing but the clothes on my back and used my suitcase for a pillow. I awoke to a new day with a new challenge.

In order to conserve money for transportation, I had not been spending money on food. I was beginning to weaken.

As I approached the French immigration officials at the border of Côte D'Ivoire, I thought I heard their instructions incorrectly.

"Excuse me?" I asked, "I'd just like to cross the border. Did you say I have to pay?"

I had not misunderstood. Each person crossing into Côte d'Ivoire was expected to pay 1000 CFA for an entry stamp. When I politely explained I had no money, expecting to be shown some sympathy or civility, I was surprised to be rudely shoved into the corner for the second time on this journey.

"Without paying the fee, you do not cross the border!" a border official shrieked.

It was not the law that was driving this policy, but greed and corruption. There was nothing I could do but watch people come and go, pay and pass by, while I was detained for hours.

"Please," I implored, "I am a preacher on my way to Sierra Leone to spread the gospel."

An angry stare from an official.

"Please, let me go," I prayed.

"Shut up! Preacher! No money, no entry!" His heart was very hard. He reminded me of Pharaoh, who wouldn't listen to Moses. My woozy head and stomach throbbed with hunger. More people paid and passed as the hours ticked by. Finally at closing time, a police boss came in and saw me sitting in the corner.

"What are you doing here?" he asked.

I explained to him that because I had no money, I had been kept there all day without being allowed to enter the country. I let him know that I knew the law. He stared at me, then went to the other officials and held a hushed consultation. A moment later, he returned and gruffly demanded my passport. Without another word, he stamped it firmly and waved me through.

I arranged for transportation to Côte D'Ivoire's capital city of Abidjan at the cost of 60 CFA, so I had to find a way to raise the moneys. I slipped the last clean suit out of my suitcase and offered to sell it to passersby. Unfortunately, it wasn't worth enough to bring the 60 CFA I needed. I was wearing my nicest suit, hoping it would survive the trip for my arrival in Sierra Leone, but I was forced to change my clothes in order to sell the more valuable suit I was wearing, securing my seat on the bus to Abidjan. The Lord was humbling me.

Now in Abidjan, I had no idea what to do next. It was my first time in a big city. I stared at the crowds and traffic bustling around me, and pondered my next step. My judgment was becoming cloudy from lack of food, I was out of money, and I had no more clothes to sell for my next bus fare. I found a place to sit down and pray to the Lord for direction.

*Trust in the LORD with all thine heart; and
lean not unto thine own understanding. In all
thy ways acknowledge him, and he shall direct
thy paths (Proverbs 3:5-6).*

I sold my watch to buy food. With a clear head, I could now
receive counsel from the Lord. He reminded me that I knew an
Aunty who had come to Nigeria some years ago, and who now
lived in Abidjan in Abromacotee. I remembered hearing her
speak of Superior Kiosk, so I called a taxi and gave the driver the
well-known location, and we arrived there without incident. It
was a journey of faith, because with no money to my name, I
prayed that my Aunty still lived there, that she was home, and
that she would welcome a destitute relative who arrived unan-
nounced with an unpaid taxi fare on her doorstep. When we
pulled up to the Kiosk, I asked for her, and neighbors pointed
out her house to me. I knocked at the door with the taxi driver's
eyes studying my back, and I thought, "If she is not here and
happy to see me, I'm going to be in big trouble with this man."

A women whose face I instantly recognized as my father's
sister opened the door. At first puzzled by the unexpected vis-
itor standing on her doorstep. She took a step back as the
shock of recognition overtook her. "Isaac, is that you?"

"Yes, it is me," I replied in relief and happiness. She
hugged me and kissed me. "Oh, God," I said softly, "thank
you for leading me here." I told her about the unpaid taxi, and
she paid the driver for me. Once again, I saw that because I
had taken a step to do God's will, He honored my faith and
made a way for me to continue.

This city of Abidjan, Côte d'Ivoire was a turning point in my journey to Sierra Leone. My Aunty gave me a place to stay, good food to eat, and much love and support. It was a great temptation to relax and enjoy her gracious hospitality permanently. After I had rested for a week, we sat together to discuss my plans.

"What are you going to do?" my Aunty asked.

"I want to continue my journey to Sierra Leone,"

"I don't want you to go," she said, "because it is obviously too dangerous to go to a place where you don't know anybody. Stay with me here and look for a job to do. Or if you choose to go home, I can put you on a flight back home to Nigeria."

My Aunt's kindness and love were welcome gifts, but I was determined not to lose my focus toward the goal of preaching in Sierra Leone. As much as I missed my family, I could not go back. All my desire was to get to my destination, no matter what it took.

"Do you know of any church in Abidjan, Aunty?" Because I need a place to preach. I believe God will use the people to bless me, so I can continue my journey."

She took me to a retired pastor and introduced me as an evangelist. The seventy-five-year-old man welcomed me, grabbed me by my shoulder, knelt me down, and began to pray for me. For half an hour I knelt before him as he praised God and thanked Him for sending this young man to him, then prayed for my protection and strength. Finally, he ended his prayer and I rose from my knees.

"So, young man, tell me about yourself," the old pastor quizzed.

I explained my mission to Sierra Leone. He told me that before I continued my journey, God first wanted to use me in Côte D'Ivoire. I was so excited to think that now, for the first time since my divine calling, somebody had accepted me as a preacher.

"Young man," said the pastor, "I want to introduce you to the church elders."

"When?"

"You come to me every day, and when you are ready, I will introduce you."

Eagerly I obeyed. Every day I reported to the old pastor for Bible study, and learned so many new things. I cleaned his house, ran his errands, performed daily household chores, and generally served him in exchange for the knowledge he shared with me. More than two months had gone by since our introduction.

"Pastor, am I ready to meet the elders?"

He studied me carefully. "Yes, I am ready to take you to the church, because I see that you are a young man with patience, and your patience will be a great blessing to you. When God called you, you needed to learn how to wait patiently for what He is going to do in your life to come to pass."

I learned obedience and patience during that time at the hands of a wise old pastor who could see these character traits were missing in my nature.

> *If ye be willing and obedient, ye shall eat the good of the land (Isaiah 1:19).*

When I arrived at the church, I saw it was a big building capable of accommodating about a hundred people. Coconut palm trees surrounded the beautiful beach-side area of Abidjan. There to meet me were five elders, who greeted me warmly with an introduction from the old pastor.

"We've heard so much about you," they said in turn.

"Thank you," I replied, "I've been very eager to meet you and begin preaching."

They nodded and smiled. Five nodding, smiling faces. The old pastor spoke for the group, "We've been very eager for you to begin preaching, too. I believe you are ready."

"Thank you. This is a nice big church. How many members do you have?"

They looked at each other in turn, then back at me. "Five," said the old pastor.

I was speechless for a moment. I looked around at the empty interior. "Five? Five members of this church?"

They nodded. "It's just us."

"Where are the other members?"

They shrugged. Sometime in the past, the church had a problem and most of the members left. No one knew exactly why, and no one knew what to do about it. So the church stood empty with only five elders and no congregation.

Since I didn't have much experience preaching, I went to the beach to study the scriptures and to practice putting my thoughts into words. I preached to anyone who went by, and sometimes I preached to the sea, the sand, and the rocks. I preached every day to the salty air, for six, even seven hours on end, until my voice was too hoarse to squeak out another word. After sunset, I went out into the city to invite people off the streets to come to the church.

"Come to church this Sunday," I told them, "You'll hear a great sermon."

Every day I practiced, and every Sunday I preached. Every day I prayed and studied, and my dear Aunty kept feeding me and caring for me. As time went on and the strength of my knowledge and confidence grew, I began to feel a change. Membership in the church was growing, and the Lord was working miracles in their lives. Many sick people were healed, and the testimony of the power of God spread like wildfire in the community. In two months, the church grew to over one hundred members. Most of the members were Ghanaian foreigners; a few were Ivorian inhabitants

One of the elders was formerly the Minister of Education in Ghana. Elder Boiton became my manager and advisor. He introduced me to other churches where I also ministered. One of the biggest churches I went to was the Apostolic Church of Christ, a denomination with over twenty branches across Côte D'Ivoire. There I met the president, Apostle Japi John.

At the end of the third month, I knew it was time for me to move on. I had witnessed a great manifestation of the Lord's spirit unfolding through my ministry in that church, but my calling was in another place. My vision had shown my feet coming to rest at the end of the map, in Sierra Leone.

We shared a tearful goodbye. The congregation came together to give me a send-off celebration service, and presented me with a love offering to see me on my journey. As I departed, I was filled with gratitude for my Aunty, the old pastor, the elders, and the church members for everything I had learned and been given during my stay in Abidjan.

I arrived at the pre-arranged location with suitcase in hand and paid for passage on a 12-passenger van that would leave at 6:00 p.m. to the city of Danane in Guinea. I had researched the route I would follow, the stopping points, and the cost for each segment of the way, and I had money in my pocket to pay for my travel. I was truly blessed.

The departure time was delayed until 8:00 p.m. I fidgeted anxiously for two hours.

Uneasy, I boarded a bus without any female passenger. In Africa, traveling in the company of all men is a sign of potential danger. As I entered the van and saw the criminal appearance of the men sitting in the other seats, I was tempted to turn around and go back to my Aunt's house, back to the old pastor and the elders, to the congregation of faithful members who loved me and wanted me as their preacher. But I knew there was no possibility of getting a refund for my fare.

If the Lord wanted me to go to Sierra Leone, He would protect and deliver me. I took my seat and bowed my head in prayer, where I stayed for most of the trip.

As we approached Danane, I raised my head in relief and prepared to get off. I looked out the windows and watched the city lights go by, and turned my attention to the bus I would be taking from Danane to the border of Guinea and Sierra Leone. It was midnight; not many people were out on the streets. The van made a turn and drove through another section of the city, leaving the main streets behind. My grip on the suitcase handle tightened. We appeared to be leaving the city and heading toward Liberia.

"Stop!" I cried in alarm. "This is the wrong way. I need to get off here in Danane."

The driver kept driving. He said something to one of the other men in a language I did not understand.

"Stop the van!" I insisted. "I am not going to Liberia: I am going to Sierra Leone and I need to go through Danane. We've passed the city already."

I tried to get out of the van, but the men surrounding me pushed me back down in my seat. Although I couldn't understand what they were saying to each other, I did understand that they had plans for me, and I could only worry in silence as the city lights retreated behind me in the distance. We drove for some time out into the countryside, where there were no houses and no electricity. It was a thick darkness without a single light to pierce it but our headlights. Suddenly, the van stopped.

"You!" one of the men shouted at me in English, "Come down here!"

I refused. We were in the middle of nowhere, in the middle of the night, in a foreign country. I was sitting in my only hope of transportation.

"You!" he shouted again, "Get out!"

Again I refused, so they pulled me from my seat and pushed me out the door onto the road. My suitcase landed in the dirt next to me.

"What am I supposed to do here?" I protested. "I am trying to get through Danane to Sierra Leone, and you have taken me far from where I need to go."

They gestured ahead down the road in the direction they were traveling. "Follow this way," they said. "In a short distance you will come to a small town. You will find transportation there." They laughed and shut the door, then drove away.

I stood in the darkness, watching the last red glow of their taillights disappear. I knew we had traveled some way from Danane, but I didn't know how far. I weighed the wisdom of following the advice of bad men who had just abandoned me in the middle of nowhere, but reasoned that I must be nearing a town of some kind if I continued onward as they had suggested. It occurred to me that if they had wanted to rob me, they would have taken my money, and they certainly wouldn't throw my suitcase to me before they took off. I decided to take my chances continuing towards Liberia.

I had walked for about five minutes, letting my eyes adjust to the darkness, when I noticed a figure standing by the roadside in an extremely dark place. My breath quickened. Who was this person? His apparel was different in some way that I could not put my finger on. Every step closer brought the scripture pounding harder in my heart:

> *The LORD is my shepherd; I shall not want. He maketh me to lie down in green pastures: he leadeth me beside the still waters.He restoreth my soul: he leadeth me in the paths of righteousness for his name's sake. Yea, though I walk through the valley of the shadow of death, I will fear no evil: for thou art with me; thy rod and thy staff they comfort me. Thou preparest a table before me in the presence of mine enemies: thou anointest my head with oil; my cup runneth over. Surely goodness and mercy shall follow me all the days of my life: and I will dwell in the house of the LORD for ever (Psalms 23).*

I was walking on the other side of the road, as far from strangers as possible. As I passed him, he called out to me, "Young man, stop!" I walked faster, fearful of an encounter on that dark country road. He followed me and asked me to stop a second time. I walked even faster, gripping the handle of my suitcase firmly and trying to think of some way to defend myself.

A third time he said, "Stop walking that way' you are going in the wrong direction." I wondered how he could know what direction I should be going.

"I am here to help you. Don't be afraid," he said in an unusually calm and reassuring way.

For some reason I no longer felt afraid. I stopped. I stood still. The Word of God came to me:

> *For God hath not given us the spirit of fear;*
> *but of power, and of love, and of a sound mind*
> *(2 Timothy 1:7).*

I drew strength from the scripture playing in my heart: even if I walk through the shadow of death, I shall fear no evil, because the Lord is with me.

The stranger drew near.

"What can I do for you?" I asked him.

"I am not here to harm you. I am here to help you," he said.

"What do you want?"

"To take you to safety. You are going the wrong way," he insisted.

"How do you know?"

"There is a checkpoint up ahead. They will pass through in their van without suspicion. They need you to also pass through the checkpoint unharmed, with your belongings and your identification papers intact. Then when you are on foot they will ambush you. They plan to kill you and use you as a sacrifice. They have killed many people in this area, like this, in the middle of the night. The people in that van are cannibals."

I was stunned to hear these words. "But how do you know this? And what brings you here in the middle of the night, in the middle of nowhere?"

"I have come to help you because you are an evangelist."

"How do you know that I am an evangelist?"

"God knows everyone who belongs to Him" the man replied. "God knows His messengers and you are one of them. I will take you to a place where you are going to sleep this night and tomorrow morning you can continue your journey."

"How do you know I am traveling?"

"You are going to Sierra Leone," he replied.

"How do you know that I am going to Sierra Leone? I don't know you. Who informed you about me or my plans?"

He did not answer my questions. He had already answered them. He reached out his hand. "Give me your suitcase. Let me help you; you are tired."

He took my suitcase from me and we turned back on the road to Danane. During the two hours we walked together, I asked him about many things. "What language do you speak? Why do you speak English when everybody here speaks French or their local language?"

"I speak all languages," he stated simply.

I wondered how he knew everything about my destination, and me, when I hadn't talked to anybody on the way. "What is your name?' I asked, but he didn't answer. "Do you have a name?" I pressed him. "I am," he replied. We walked on in silence. He seemed content just to remove me from that dangerous place and see me to safety.

In the early hours of the morning, when I felt I was walking in my sleep, he brought me to a church in Danane and knocked on the door. When the door was opened, he said, "This young man is tired. You have two rooms that nobody is occupying. Let him rest in one of your rooms before he continues his journey."

Without argument, they agreed and opened their guest quarters to me. The stranger entered with me and set down my suitcase. "You are safe here. Rest and continue your journey when day breaks. God be with you, Isaac," he said. Then he left and closed the door. Wild with curiosity, I opened the door and followed him out. I had many questions about this man of whom I knew so little and yet who seemed to know so much about me.

As I watched him walk away, all of a sudden he disappeared, and I felt something cool enter my body. I began to weep. God had sent His messenger that night to guide and protect me. I would have been killed in that place, if God had not sent His angel to lead me to safety. This was the fulfillment of the Word of God in my life.

> *For he shall give his angels charge over thee, to*
> *keep thee in all thy ways (Psalm 91:11).*

The next morning, I was refreshed by a wonderful sleep. I thanked the people who had been hospitable to me, and continued my journey. At the bus station, I was asked by Guinean border police to declare any money I was carrying. They said it was their procedure: I must sign a paper stating how much money I brought into their country. I held out all the money I had.

"Do you have a paper proving that you can carry this money with you?" The border policeman asked.

"I am an evangelist and a preacher, and the money was given to me as a love offering from the church where I worked in Abidjan."

"Oh, I see," said the policeman, "so you earned this money working at a church."

"I am not a businessman, only a preacher. This money was given to me to do the Lord's work."

"Well, if you cannot show a paper proving it is rightfully yours, then you are not allowed to carry it in our country." said the Guinean policeman as he confiscated it. He counted out just enough money to pay for my transport from Danane to the Sierra Leone border. But that would not be the end of my journey. From the border I still had to traverse the entire country to the western seaport of Freetown.

"If you take that money from me, then you are thieves. You have to give me my money back!" I angrily shouted.

They threatened to arrest me if I did not leave peacefully. Naïve to corruption and unprepared for the schemes of wicked men, I had walked blindly into their trap. If I fought back, I could be detained. If I went forward, I would once again be stranded with no money to complete my journey. Having faith that the Lord would provide a way for me in the wilderness, I picked up my luggage, entered the bus, and left Guinea.

The next morning, our bus arrived in Sierra Leone. Crossing the border into Sierra Leone gave me a great sense of achievement, and I said a silent prayer of thanks for my safe journey so far. However, that was not the final destination. I continued on the same bus to the town of Koidu, where I was forced to disembark for lack of funds. The three-day trip from Koidu to Freetown would cost three thousand Leone, an impossible sum for me. I investigated further.

The only transportation available from Koidu to the neighboring town of Kenema was to ride with farmers driving their coco to market in large trailers. These trailers didn't run every day, and after seeing the amount of coco loaded on the truck, I wondered how any people could possibly fit. The coco entirely filled the trailer, and then the passengers climbed to the top of the load and sat on the coco. I learned that in Kenema there would be better transportation available, but without the money to travel even that far, it did me little good.

I sat down in one of the coco stores to meditate, think and pray a practice that I had occupied myself with during most of the trip. I praised God for every move and step I took, and had courage that God would use me according to the vision, because I was now on the soil of Sierra Leone.

"Excuse me, sir," I asked a man, "is there any church around here?"

"No, he said, "there is no church. Almost everyone in this town is a Muslim. Are you a Christian?"

"I am."

After a while, another man came to me.

"I understand that you are looking for a church," he said politely.

"Yes, I am."

He continued. "I know one man who is a Christian, if you are interested in speaking to him."

"Sure."

As we walked through the streets, the man told me this Christian owned one of the largest coco shops in that area. My guide took me to him, introduced us, told the Christian farmer that I had traveled all the way from Nigeria, and that I was looking for a church.

The farmer shook my hand and welcomed me. He gave me a cup of water to drink as a sign of welcome and told me he was born in Nigeria but had lived almost all his life in Sierra Leone. He went on to say there was no church in Koidu; in order to attend church services he had to travel to a big city. After I explained my mission to Freetown, he encouraged me to stay with him and rest until one of his coco trailers was traveling to Freetown. He offered to arrange passage for me on his trailer. I related the story of the Guinea border police stealing my money, and he told me not to worry. He promised to pay my transport to Freetown. I thanked him very much for helping me, and we prayed together. He provided me with a place to sleep at his house that night, and the next evening we went to the park where the coco was loaded. The man paid for my ticket and also gave me some extra money, for which I was extremely grateful.

The truck was fully loaded, and from my vantage point looking up at the mountain of coco, I could not see a single space for a human being to sit. The workers were used to that, and knew exactly what to do from their experience. Like acrobats, they swung themselves up onto the truck and began jumping up and down to pack the load, then extended a hand to each passenger to help them to the top of the coco. There we were, perched precariously in an open truck, free to slip and slide on the shifting load with every bump and pothole. We held on for dear life to avoid the risk of falling out, especially going up and down steep hills, around sharp corners, and over rocks and through mud holes. We were sure the truck would tip and dump us over the sheer drop next to the narrow, winding road. As we traveled west through the night, afraid to fall asleep for fear of releasing our handhold and falling out, it began to rain. Suddenly from the darkness, my face was slashed by a passing tree branch so hard it knocked my head back. I felt my cheek and found it wet with blood.

The sun broke over the eastern horizon behind us as we stopped in a small town for gas and food. It was our first stop all night, and our first opportunity to get down and stretch our cramped legs and backs. My face was swollen, my arms were tired from holding on, and my eyes were bloodshot from lack of sleep, but I was happily covering the miles that took me closer to the mission for which God had called me.

CHAPTER FOUR
THE DREAM WORLD

CHAPTER FOUR
THE DREAM WORLD

For three days we traveled on the coco truck across Sierra Leone toward the coast, through open countryside and small towns, farms, jungle, bush, rain, shine, mud and dust. I can't really say I saw much of the scenery, as I was looking at the sky or bowing my head in prayer for most of the way. When I climbed down stiffly and waited for the felling to return to my legs, I was covered in dust from head to toe. The blood on my cheek was dried and open to infection, and I had slept very little since leaving Koidu.

I was the most blessed man on earth. I had arrived.

God had called me to this country, and had made it possible to deliver me safely. It was a dream come true. Many people told me it would be impossible, but because of my faith and a willingness to keep going, I stood in the unreal world I had seen in my vision. The discouragement and disparaging advice from people who said I could never make it melted away. I had carried the vision inside of me across five countries, and no one could understand the great relief I felt as my feet touched the ground in Freetown. There was no one there to welcome me, so I took a moment to welcome myself and enjoy my achievement: "Welcome to the land of vision."

Now all I needed to do was secure food, lodging, and a place to begin my mission of preaching to the multitudes. I looked all around. I didn't know where to go or where to start, so I walked to the center of Freetown to see the city. It was bigger than the villages in the surrounding countryside, with more buildings and cars and pedestrians crowding the markets. Men and women carried loads of merchandise on their heads, in carts, and on bicycles. Traffic was crazy mix of private cars, taxis and buses going every direction without any rhyme or reason, and seemingly without any traffic laws. This was a poor city, dirty, primitive in construction and commerce, and the recent rains had turned the dirt streets to mud.

It was July 1991, the middle of the rainy season in West Africa, which would bring three months of heavy rains, thunder, and lightning strong enough to cut off trees.

I walked into a hotel hoping to rent a room, but learned I could not even afford a single night. I thought perhaps the Nigerian embassy might help one of its citizens in need, so I inquired there if they would help me find a place to stay. They informed me they were not responsible for finding accommodations for people, but they were prepared to send me back home to Nigeria if I declared I was stranded.

"Stranded?" I protested. "I've just arrived, and I haven't done what I came to do."

"What are you here to do?" the embassy staff member inquired.

"I am here on a mission to preach the gospel."

There was one Nigerian man, he explained, who might help me find accommodation.

With his address in hand and directions from the embassy, I went in search of my fellow countryman, Mr. Pa Kayode. I arrived at a mechanic's workshop and looked over the automobile parts and tires stacked on the property. Oil and grease stained the ground black. My introduction had become well rehearsed by now: God had sent me there to preach the gospel, how I had traveled from Nigeria to Sierra Leone.

"Wonderful! Wonderful!" Mr. Kayode said excitedly. "I am very happy to receive you. You are welcome."

"I need a temporary place to stay until I can find a place for myself."

Suddenly his demeanor changed. "I live in a mansion," he told me, "with five large rooms. Two of them are empty."

I beamed. Now I would be in comfortable quarters.

"However," he went on, "I am not prepared to accommodate you because the God who called you should be able to take care of you. You are not welcome to live in my house."

Shock waves ran through me. I could not reconcile his apparently friendly gesture a moment ago with this sudden disdain towards me. Whatever the source of his hostility, I could not grasp what I had said or done to reverse his attitude so completely.

"Thank you for your time," I managed to say politely, then turned to leave. Outside the workshop, I sat down dejectedly on top of one of the wrecked cars and began to pray. Somehow I had to find a place to stay, something to eat, and a way to begin preaching. A few minutes later, someone called to me.

"You!" Mr. Kayode shouted, "I can see you really don't have any place to go. I want to give you some help." He looked me over intently. "If you want it."

I nodded.

"You see that blue car over there?" He pointed to an old, 1950 jacked up Mercedes Benz without engine or wheels. To call it blue was generous, as it was covered with more rust than paint. Its rotted interior still had seats, but no windows.

"My boys could clean it up for you to make it more habitable. Do you want it?"

I nodded. It was far from the lap of luxury, but after it had been cleaned it became my makeshift house: the backseat my bedroom, the front seat my living room, and the trunk my wardrobe. I was very dusty and smelly from my journey, and had not showered in days. The mechanic suggested that I wait until nightfall to shower outside in an open place, because without electricity the whole city would be blacked out.

That night, I discreetly bathed in the darkness of the junkyard, climbed into the car, and slept peacefully for the first time since the church in Danane.

The next morning, I had many questions for this Nigerian mechanic about my new city. Mr. Kayode told me this was Freetown, city of darkness, a city that had been without electricity for twenty-five years. According to the garage owner, from the time the present government of President Joseph Momoh took control from the former president, Shaken Steven, the city had been without electricity.

More questions, more prayer. What was God's purpose for me? God wanted to use me to transform Sierra Leone. With a population in the capital city of about a million people, there were only fifty Pentecostal churches; the largest congregation was about twenty-five members. Day after day was spent visiting each church in turn, walking through the streets in the rain, talking with the pastors and explaining my calling from the Lord. One by one, the pastors refused to receive me and accused me of being a false prophet.

"I know there are false prophets all over the world, but I am not one of them. The Lord told me to come here. I saw it very clearly in my vision."

The pastors communicated among themselves, warning each other to turn away the newcomer with such big ideas. They sent a message that I should leave the city, because I would not be allowed to preach there. The Bible says if you go into a place and they refuse you, you should dust off your feet and leave.

*And whosoever shall not receive you, nor hear
your words, when ye depart out of that house or
city, shake off the dust of your feet. Verily I say
unto you, It shall be more tolerable for the land
of Sodom and Gomorrha in the day of judgment, than for that city (Matthew 10:14-15).*

In spite of what the Bible says, I stayed in Freetown. God
had not sent me to the pastors. He had sent me to the dying
souls in the darkness of Freetown. It was not the people who
refused me, but the pastors. They told me to stop going to
churches, so I returned to my Mercedes Benz house to meditate and pray for a way to accomplish the Lord's mission. I
could lay down curled up in the back seat or sit in the front seat,
but when the cold rain fell it leaked everywhere. Between rain-
storms I dried the seats off and welcomed the chance to sleep
warmly, though then plagued by flies and mosquito's. I salvaged
a dirty cup from the yard and cleaned it of engine oil, washed
it, and placed it on top of the car to catch rainwater to drink.

In the early days of my stay in the junkyard, the garage
owner occasionally came by to ask how I was doing and give
me some bread. But eventually, even he abandoned me. I had
not a soul to turn to for help in this strange city, and I cried
bitterly to God. I was so dry and skinny that I thought I
would die. Over thirty days had passed since I had eaten. One
afternoon, so tired and weak that standing was difficult, I
struggled to my feet and made my way to the mango tree by
the workshop. The small fruit hanging there were green, but
in my desperation I ate some to fill my aching hunger. Within
minutes my stomach began to hurt so much that I rolled on

the ground in pain, crying and praying, "Oh God, help me." Then as suddenly as the pain hit me, it left.

Unbeknownst to me, there were eyes on me, observing my unusual actions. They saw a tall, dusty, emaciated man sitting in a junkyard car, waiting for nightfall to wash himself and his one set of clothes, and waiting for them to dry with a towel wrapped around his waist. They watched this madman eat unripe fruit, yell and roll in the dirt, then crawl back to his car in the rain. Silent neighbors added another crazy behavior to the already strange list of things they had seen and heard coming from inside the auto mechanic's fence.

Time began to blur. Weeks passed. I was so thin that the bones in my face were visible just beneath my skin. One late afternoon, the clouds cleared and the sun warned the roof of my makeshift abode. In my weakened state, near starvation and exhausted from endless rainy nights without sleep, I crawled out to sit on the trunk and bask in the brightness of a rare sunny day. On my lap was my Bible, opened to Matthew's prophetic account of the second coming of Jesus Christ. So engrossed were my thoughts in the fascinating scripture that I did not notice people quietly drawing close around me. They looked at me warily, puzzled at my intense focus on the book in my lap. When I lifted my eyes, there were nearly thirty people staring expectantly at me. No one spoke, just gazed at me, waiting for me to do something funny.

Finally, I broke the silence. "How can I help you? What do you want?"

They looked at each other and tried to decide how to handle the curious situation.

"If you think I am crazy, you are wrong," I said. "I am not crazy. I am a preacher, an evangelist sent here by God to preach His Gospel. I am just living here for the meantime."

They were surprised to hear me speak so intelligently. One stepped forward and asked me, "tell us what you are reading."

Taking up the challenge, I began to explain Matthew 24 to the onlookers: how Jesus Christ sat on the Mount of Olives and the disciples came to Him privately to ask about the signs of His coming. The Lord told the disciples there would be rumors of wars, and wars in different countries; the signs of the second coming of Christ; events that would usher in His coming. This prophesies I shared with my band of skeptical onlookers, and related the Biblical description of the Lord appearing in a cloud with the sound of a trumpet, with the faithful saints around Him in the air. In great detail, I explained what I was reading and what it meant. The power of God came down and touched some of the crowd, and there was a great manifestation of His anointing.

There, perched on the dilapidated shell of an abandoned car, in the evening light of a mechanic's yard, I received my first opportunity to preach to the people of Sierra Leone. There was no big hall, no lights flashing around, no music piped over loudspeakers, no fancy clothes or announcements, only the simple truth of the Gospel told by a man named

Matthew. Like me, he had a story to tell of his Lord and Savior, Jesus Christ.

Among the people present that day was an advance man with a Bible in his hand, a man who was to be the instrument God would use in my life. After listening intently to every word I said, the man approached me.

"Young man, where are you from?"

"I am from Nigeria."

"How long have you been here?"

"I am here now for three months."

"Where do you live?"

"This is my house-the car that I was sitting on."

"I know the owner of this workshop," he said. "He could not give you a place to live?"

"No, but he gave me this place to live, and I am grateful for that."

"Let me be honest with you," he continued. "I am a pastor, and I have never heard anyone explain Matthew 24 about the coming of Christ the way you have just explained it. Sunday is our church service. Can you come and preach to us? I want to request that you preach the same message to the people."

"Alright."

The first door was opened to preach in a Freetown church. Rev. James Gober of the "Joy Assemblies of God" welcomed me to join his flock, and my heart was filled with gratitude and relief for the end of my ordeal.

On Sunday, it was an effort to dress myself and travel the short distance to the church. In my faltering state I wondered if I would make it, but I knew I had to be there for this long-awaited opportunity. When I arrived, the service was already in progress and I waited until the pastor invited me to come and preach, then began teaching from Matthew 24 as he had requested, in the same manner as my impromptu open-air sermon earlier that week. I soon forgot my pain and felt the joy and peace of speaking God's Word. To my surprise, many church members wept. The realization struck me that unlike my country where churches filled with believers numbered in the thousands, this church in Sierra Leone held a mere twenty-five people and was one of the largest churches in the city. The outpouring of the Holy Spirit touched their hearts, and afterwards the pastor gave me a love offering that meant I would be able to buy food.

Later at Rev. Gober's home, I was cautious about eating after my extended fast. The last escapade with unripe mango fruit was still fresh in my memory, so I asked for some bread and hot tea. That was my first meal in over thirty days, and it was as welcome as the most wonderful feast. I rested at the pastor's house. When I was ready, I told him I was going home.

"Home?" He asked, "What home? You don't have a home."

"But you met me somewhere. That was my home in the car garage."

I felt insulted because he said I did not have a home. Actually, that was true. My temperament was such that I did not want anybody to use my situation to insult me.

Tears welled in my eyes as I cast my mind back on all that I had been through.

"Do not cry," Rev. Gober comforted. "We are going to help you."

"Have I been brought to your house to insult me because I don't have a decent home?"

My continuing situation had made me easily irritated in spite of the pastor's good intentions. Laughing had become a thing of the past. There was no humor left in me, only sensitivity.

"I am sorry," he soothed. "I did not mean to hurt your feelings." Rev. Gober wisely knew not to take my crankiness personally, that when a person has been hurt or been through a difficult time, what they need is patience and lots of love. The fault is not theirs, even though they can be very difficult. People in this state feel they are not well treated, and oftentimes become hard to please even in the midst of honest effort by well-meaning friends and family. With prayers and acceptance from loving people, they begin to change.

Rev. Gober asked me to wait, so I consented to stay a bit more. An assistant, Pastor Karim Koroma, was introduced as my host, who led me to his apartment and gave me a simple furnished room in which to live. For the first time in three months, I slept in a real bed with my legs stretched to their full length. When I awoke feeling rested, warm and dry, I knelt to thank the Lord for His blessings. This would be my home for a couple of months, where I had the opportunity to work in the church.

However, in spite of moving from the abandoned car to a proper house, my weeks of unhealthy exposure had taken their toll. I had contracted malarial fever and for two weeks found myself unable to stand up from the bed or hold any food in my stomach. Rev. Gober urged me to seek a doctor's attention, but I was aware of the unprofessional standard of medical care in Sierra Leone, where patients were often misdiagnosed or mistreated and became even worse. Despite my firm belief in proper medical care and medications, I still believed that at that time, God's divine healing was the only way I would recover.

Rev. Gober became increasingly alarmed as my illness progressed. He pleaded with me, if not for my own sake, for the sake of the church. If I died in his hands, the church would suffer negative consequences. He went to the Nigerian embassy. There he was told there was a record of my arrival in the country as a preaching evangelist, and that if my condition had not improved in one week, they would pick me up and send me back to Nigeria for proper treatment.

I protested. After all I had been through to get to Sierra Leone, I was not going back home without accomplishing the mission the Lord had sent me to do. The embassy's twofold concern was simple: I was taking a risk with my life, and I was unable to fend for myself or find work as a sick man. I assured them that the Lord would heal me, and not to worry, because God is the Lord who heals. He is greater than the greatest physician in the world, and can move in one's life according to a person's responses of faith.

Rolling slowly out of bed, I knelt down and rested my head against the sheets. After praying to God for healing, I fell into a deep and long sleep. In the afternoon, one of the pastors knocked at the door to check on my condition. When I got up to open the door, I realized I was completely healed. I jumped as if I had never been sick. The Lord had healed me!

This miracle of God was soon told to others, and to others, each time by dumbfounded witnesses, astounded at my recovery without medical aid.

CHAPTER FIVE
THE SITUATION CHANGED

CHAPTER FIVE
THE SITUATION CHANGED

After my miraculous recovery, the pastor with whom I was living asked me what my plans were.

"I want to organize a prayer conference."

"You could do it in the church," he offered.

I politely declined. "The church hall is too small; it can only hold twenty-five people. I need a bigger space."

"Why?"

"I need to rent a big hall to hold all the people."

He was puzzled. "They do not hold big programs in Freetown. People will not attend," the pastor explained.

"How many people live in Freetown?"

"More than one million people."

"I have faith to move crowds, because I believe in my vision of preaching to a multitude of people, and I expect it to happen."

The conference hall I rented was inexpensive, and could accommodate a thousand people. The Lord planted the idea in my mind to bring people together in a prayer conference to break the powers of darkness, and bring light and revival to the nation. The conference was planned to last five days. It was June, 1992, and I believed the people were ready for a change in their lives.

> *For the earnest expectation of the creature waiteth for the manifestation of the sons of God (Romans 8:19).*

The first day of the prayer conference brought only 100 people. When I ministered, the power of God came down, and the Holy Spirit touched everyone present. I could see the people of Freetown were so hungry for God, and were waiting to see this manifestation. The first evening, people were falling under the Power of God. Sick people were healed. Day two and three continued with miracles of healing, and the numbers of people attending grew. By the fourth day, the meeting had already been recorded at the largest gathering of believers in Freetown. The pastors had never seen anything of this magnitude. To me it was just the beginning.

On the fourth day, some people shared their testimonies of the various healings they had experienced. When the time came for me to preach, I went up and took the microphone.

"The power of God is going to come down here tonight. Would everybody please stand."

Directly before me in the front row, a boy remained in his seat. I came down from the stage, went to the boy, held his hand, and lifted him up. He stood.

"Walk towards me," I invited.

The boy stepped out of his seat and started walking with me. The people on the front row began to scream and clap. I did not understand the sudden excitement until I was told the reason for their amazement: the boy could not stand, much less walk. He was paralyzed. The miracle of Adeyemi Ladna's healing electrified the atmosphere.

"We have never seen a thing like that before," everyone said. People began leaving the hall to call their friends and families to come and witness the healing power of God in action, much like the woman of Samaria did when Jesus Christ told her everything about her life.

> *The woman then left her waterpot, and went her way into the city, and saith to the men, Come, see a man, which told me all things that ever I did: is not this the Christ? Then they went out of the city, and came unto him (John 4:28-30).*

The miracles in this meeting were phenomenal. On the last day of the conference, more people than ever were drawn to the full house. The media, mainly the radio, carried the news across the country, most especially about the healing ministry of the powerful evangelist, Isaac Dennis.

One day, my team members brought a message of a man who had heard about me on the radio broadcast while lying in a hospital bed. Paralyzed by a stroke, he had been unable to move for six months. After hearing all the testimonies on the radio, he developed a strong faith that if this man Isaac Dennis came and prayed for him, he would be healed.

When I heard the message, I was hesitant. The man's condition was deplorable. Unable to stand up, move his body, or even turn in the bed without help, he had little hope of recovery. I was afraid that if I went to the hospital, prayed for his healing, and his condition did not improve, the media might broadcast this bad news and the image of my ministry would crumble.

For more than three weeks, the man's family and my own team members continually urged me to go to him. They were relentless in their insistence, and I was wearing out. It was such a disturbing decision, one that could not be made without praying for the Lord's guidance. One day, my team returned with news that the man kept asking for me repeatedly. If this man believed so strongly in my prayer of faith, the Lord would honor his faith. We went to the hospital.

The crowded hospital room housed about fifteen patients. Along with their reputation for substandard medical care, Freetown hospitals frequently accommodate twenty or more people in one room. There lay the man in his bed, unaware of the identity of his visitors. Although he had heard me on the radio, he had not seen my picture. Approaching his bedside, I asked if I could pray for him.

"No," said the man. "It is Isaac Dennis I want to pray for me."

"OK, if it is Isaac Dennis you want, you wait until he comes." I turned to leave.

As I walked away, the man's brother told him, "That is Isaac Dennis."

He shouted, "Please, sir, I am sorry. I didn't know it was you."

I went back, convinced he really had faith in my prayer. As I drew near, he tried to lift up his hand, but he could not move. When I saw that, I was moved with compassion and laid both hands on him. During my prayer for his recovery, his bones began making cracking noises all over his body. Healing was taking place. At the end of the prayer, he responded to my request to stand up by sitting on his bed. He said the tubes connected to him were preventing him from walking, so I told the attending nurse and doctor to remove the tubes. They witnessed the miracle of healing unfolding, but they were stupefied, so I put my hand on the tube, pulled it out, and asked the man to stand up and walk. He did. After six months of lying paralyzed in bed, he got to his feet and walked all around the hall. The other sick people in the room received prayers for healing before I left that day.

Two days passed before I returned to visit the patients to see how they were recovering, expecting to find their conditions improving. I walked in to find an empty room. The nurse told me they had all gone home, because they were healed. This culmination of our first prayer conference gave me added confidence and faith in the power of the Lord's mission for me in Sierra Leone.

Tremendous results also followed in other cities across the provinces, where large multitudes responded to announcements of my prayer meetings. As the first evangelist to conduct miracle crusades across the nation, I became well known for the healing power of prayer. Many crusade converts became pastors and evangelists, and churches started to grow in large numbers. People sometimes stopped me in the street to share their story of conversion at one of my crusades, and their entry into the ministry. There is still so much joy in hearing these testimonies of conversions to Christ.

As an evangelist, my calling was not to remain stationary, but to continually move on to a new area. From time to time reports reached us about what happened after my departure. We planned an international crusade in the neighboring Republic of Guinea, where upon my arrival a pastor invited me to his church of about two hundred members in an Islamic-dominated stronghold. There he introduced me as the man of God whose Freetown crusade was the reason for his conversion and subsequent ministry of the Gospel. I was so excited to hear this wonderful, life-changing testimony from a man I did not even know. It was evidence of the fruit of our labors in the prayer crusades.

My next plan was to organize a citywide crusade on a football field in Freetown, Sierra Leone. I chose a football field to openly declare the power of God in a city of darkness. There, in front of an audience of more than five thousand people, I prophesied to the nation that this city, a city that had been in darkness for more than twenty-five years, was going to come into the light. I told them I was a servant of God, that God had sent me there, and at the end of the crusade there would be electricity. I told the crowd that God was going to change the government.

The week following the crusade, the military took over power from the government, and Captain Valentine Strasser became the President of Sierra Leone.

After two weeks in power, the new government announced over the radio that the generator plant was broken, and that a contact had been signed for its repair. Within the next few weeks, the announcer said, there would be electricity. Three weeks later, electric power was restored. More than one hundred thousand people left their homes to dance in the street, ecstatic over the joyous results. Sierra Leone was like a new country. Watching the fulfillment of the prophecy in Freetown, I gave praise to God for bringing to pass the dream for which I had laid down my life. My faith had become sight; my hope had become reality. God had used me to change a nation!

CHAPTER SIX
STOPPING THE POWERS

CHAPTER SIX
STOPPING THE POWERS

Now that the prophecy was fulfilled, there was more work to do. The next step was to take a spiritual stand against the satanic practices in the church. Demonic secret societies and witchcraft were openly practiced in Freetown. People wore masks and witchcraft dressings to an annual thanksgiving ceremony, and this was widely accepted in the big ancient churches. These are things that can never be accepted in the Church, but these churches opened their doors to all sorts of compromises, from moral failure to outright demon worship. They were, in essence, trying to put the Almighty God and the devil together in one worship service, an abomination of the highest order! God does not take glory in idolatry. Darkness and light cannot work together.

The practice of traditional worship mixed with demonic idolatry was so deeply rooted that no preacher could stand against it or challenge it. A headquarter for witchcraft, the entire city of Freetown was pervaded with the shadow of darkness. People died premature deaths; women became barren or died in labor; children disappeared due to human rituals; and poverty prevailed at the highest rate of any nation on earth. Seeing this in the country broke my heart.

In the heart of the city of Freetown, a football field housed regular midnight gatherings of witches. An international evangelist came from the United States to hold a crusade in that venue. The occult leaders notified him that his crusade would disturb their nightly meeting, but the evangelist felt he had strong enough power to stand against any team of witches. He instructed his technical team to mount up the speakers. The crusade was staged and ready to begin. At six that evening, the Freetown witches gathered and called up a heavy wind that blew with tornado force around the stadium. All the speakers, equipment, and even the platform flew into the air, sending people running for their lives from the crusade field. The equipment landed two miles away, and the witches came to say they warned the preacher but he wouldn't listen. The news of this terrible challenge of God's power disturbed me, so I prayed and asked God to do something about it. I called on my crusade team and discussed holding a crusade in that same football field. The venue was important as a message: to challenge the powers of the witches and demonstrate the power of Jesus Christ, because the Bible says:

> *For I am not ashamed of the gospel of Christ:*
> *for it is the power of God unto salvation to*
> *every one that believeth; to the Jew first, and*
> *also to the Greek (Romans 1:16).*

The crusade of spiritual warfare was organized to break the devil's back and bring victory over the powers of witchcraft in

Freetown. In this spiritual warfare crusade, I knew I put my life on the line, openly challenging the dark powers of the secret cult society, as Elijah did with the prophets of Baal.

> *And it came to pass at the time of the offering of the evening sacrifice, that Elijah the prophet came near, and said, Lord God of Abraham, Isaac, and of Israel, let it be known this day that thou art God in Israel, and that I am thy servant, and that I have done all these things at thy word. Hear me, O Lord, hear me, that this people may know that thou hast turned their heart back again. Then the Fire of the Lord fell and consumed the burnt sacrifice, and the wood, and the stones, and the dust, and licked up the water that was in the trench. And when all the people saw it, they fell on their faces: and they said, The Lord, He is the God; the Lord, He is the God. And Elijah said unto them, take the prophets of Baal; let not one of them escape. And they took them: and Elijah brought them down to the brook kishon, and slew them there. And Elijah said unto Ahab, get thee up, eat and drink; for there is a sound of abundance of rain (1 Kings 18:36-41).*

Until you destroy the powers of darkness that are in control of a city, town, or village, you will never see progress; there will always be evil manifestation. Hence, the strategy I often deployed was to disarm the prince of darkness assigned to the city I was going to minister.

For we wrestle not against flesh and blood, but against principalities, against power, against the rules of the darkness of this world, against spiritual wickedness in high places (Ephesians 6:12).

The crusade planning went forward. As soon as the occult practitioners received our publicity, they sent me a letter asking me to change the venue, because the grounds belonged to them for their nightly meetings. I responded that from the night of my crusade, there would never be witchcraft meetings in that football field again. On the day the crusade was scheduled to begin, curious onlookers gathered to watch Isaac Dennis' speakers flying through the air. They didn't know what would happen, but they didn't want to miss the spectacle. As the opening music began, the sky suddenly darkened with gathering clouds, and wind began to blow as though heavy rain would fall. I went forward and took the microphone. Lifting my hands high, I commanded the power of the witches to be broken in the name of Jesus Christ. Within five minutes, the sky cleared, the wind stopped, and the crusade went as planned. Our victory over the powers of witchcraft was not because I was more powerful than the American evangelist; it was because I was given a special assignment and anointing from God to do that job.

One evening during a crusade, I made an altar call for the conversion of every secret cult member. After listening to a powerful message in an open-air crusade before ten thousand people, one hundred and fifty occult members gave their lives to Christ. Some of them came to the stage and made a public confession of their actions in the secret society. No longer secret, it was declared in the open air. The graphic, violent terrors described that night were worse than any horror movie. And in that moment, in that crusade, the Lord broke the power of the secret cult.

The next day was a Sunday, the last day of the crusade. By afternoon a protest was formed by the secret cult groups; people held placards reading, "Isaac Dennis must go" and "Crusade must stop." Crusade workers dressed in "Isaac Dennis Gospel Crusade" uniforms were attacked and beaten, and equipment was destroyed. As the time for the evening crusade session neared, the mass demonstration became more violent. Rev. Kingsley, the coordinator of the event, was accosted by protestors, bound, and held for questioning. Occult leaders tortured him and accused him of working for me in organizing this religious crusade. Rev. Kingsley denied all statements and maintained, "I do not know Isaac Dennis. I am not his coordinator. I came to attend the crusade just like anybody else." Finally, they released him.

This reminds me of how Peter denied Jesus. And if Jesus could be denied thrice then I could also be denied. After all, I am just a man. I am not Jesus. Jesus said if we want to follow Him we must take our cross and follow Him. Carrying our cross means that we must expect everything that happens to Jesus to happen to us. The cross is not a bed of roses.

Now Peter sat without in the palace: and a damsel came unto him, saying, Thou also wast with Jesus of Galilee.

77

*But he denied before [them] all, saying, I know
not what thou sayest.*

*But he denied before [them] all, saying, I know
not what thou sayest.*

*And after a while came unto [him] they that
stood by, and said to Peter, Surely thou also art
[one] of them; for thy speech bewrayeth thee.*

*Then began he to curse and to swear, [saying],
I know not the man. And immediately the
cock crew.*

*And Peter remembered the word of Jesus, which
said unto him, Before the cock crow, thou shalt
deny me thrice. And he went out, and wept
bitterly (Matthew 26: 69-75).*

Straight to military headquarters Rev. Kingsley went.
Determined to go forward with the crusade that evening, he
requested military security for the team of the evangelist. His
request could only be granted by President Strasser himself,
who met with Rev. Kingsley and agreed to his assessment.
Twelve soldiers were sent to guard the crusade ground, and six
soldiers picked me up in a military convoy.

When I arrived, attendance was unbelievable, the largest
crowd I had ever seen in my young life. The football field
overflowed to the street, blocking major traffic. Six soldiers
flanked the stage with me, and the others spread around the
field to maintain safety. A stone flew from the midst of the

audience and hit the banner hanging across the platform. Tension sizzled in the air. I took the microphone.

"I am not here in your country because I love to be. It is because the Lord has sent me here. This is the largest Christian gathering you have ever had, and you have gotten a new government and electricity since my arrival here.

"How many of you love light? If you do, and you have ganged up with the secret cult people to disrupt this crusade with your stones and sticks to stone this evangelist, I want you to know that Jesus Christ is the Light. Come forward and drop your stones and sticks here."

The echo of my voice hung over the crowd. Silence. Slowly, one man took a step, then another and another. Over one hundred people came forward and dropped their stones and sticks. The heap of stones was very tall. They asked me to pray for them.

That night, there was a great conversion among the people. I asked the crowd to do something unusual for me, to kneel together in silence and pray for redemption. And the assembly of people knelt down in a dusty football field in prayer for their nation. I heard many among the gathering breaking out in tears, asking God for forgiveness. At the end, we had a wonderful celebration of victory in praise and worship unto God for a successful spiritual warfare crusade.

Afterwards, President Strasser issued an order to the secret occult members to stop holding their masquerades in churches, to give reverence to the house of God. This was one of my accomplishments by the grace of God. The hopeful atmosphere of revival that prevailed in Sierra Leone under the government of President Valentine Strasser was powerful enough to change the nation.

CHAPTER SEVEN
LIVING IN DANGER

CHAPTER SEVEN
LIVING IN DANGER

I had stood against their demonic forces and prevailed. Thwarted in their attempts to stop the crusade, the occult leaders had no choice but to make plans to kill me. A woman arrived with a letter accusing me of disorganizing their activities in their own country. The letter informed me that I would be killed and my body flown back to my home country in a casket. The woman was sent back with a message to every person who had contributed to the writing of the letter: "Be ready to face the judgment of God."

Soon after this communication exchange, I was in a photo shop with my coordinator when somebody tapped his shoulder and warned him urgently, "Take him out of here right now. People are coming to attack him."

We got in the car quickly, and the driver started the car. A large rock crashed into the back window. We sped away. I was in the front seat, and could not see who had thrown the stone, but we were being chased by another car at high speed. It was several blocks before the driver evaded the other car. Luckily we escaped, but it was no longer safe for me to go out in Freetown.

Under the protection of a security guard, I grew tired of staying in the house, a captive of my own notoriety. I had no choice but to leave the country for a while to let the situation cool down.

My return fare to Nigeria was arranged. Even though the flight departed at midday, we traveled to the airport under cover of darkness to avoid the risk of attack by occultists. I bade my team goodbye and wondered how long it would be before we would see each other again.

I returned to Nigeria on a two-and-a-half-hour flight, thinking all the while of the eight-month trek that brought me to Freetown. I had lived my vision. I traveled to Sierra Leone; I preached to the multitudes. Was the Lord through with me? I marveled as the plane touched down on my native soil, and thanked God for my safe return, without a casket.

Several months' preaching in Nigeria and surrounding countries passed the time and spread the Gospel. I was invited to do a three-month Gospel tour with Apostle Japi John's Apostolic Church of Christ from Abidjan. I visited most of his branches in San Pedro, Grand Bassam, and Yamoussoukro, ending my tour in the Twenty-Five Year Convention in the city called Bassam, a few miles away from Abidjan. People came in hundreds from other branches of the denomination. And outstanding testimony of my visit occurred during the convention, where I prayed for barren women. One year later, I was invited to return and dedicate fifty babies born as a result of that blessing in a single ceremony. It was a time of joy, rejoicing and jubilating. This was my last mission in 1993 in Côte D'Ivoire.

My work in Sierra Leone was not finished. The Lord bade me return to the country of my greatest successes and most terrifying perils. Time had healed the cult leaders' memory of me, so I called together my crusade team once again. In December 1994, we filled the national stadium with over thirty-five thousand believers. There, a young boy who attended the school for deaf and mute, who had never heard nor spoken in his life, experienced a miracle of the Lord's healing. He could hear, and he could speak. He began counting, "One, two, and three." Freetown saw a miracle, and was astonished once again.

CHAPTER EIGHT
Blood in Africa

CHAPTER EIGHT
Blood in Africa

The success of my last crusade in the national stadium raised my evangelical ministry to a higher dimension and awareness than ever before. By the grace of God, I had become the spiritual head of the country, although this had never been my life's goal. My mission was to spread God's message to new places, and it was time to move on. But if I left the nation in the hands of less experience pastors, they would be without the spiritual support. They needed to take a stand against the war being waged in the provinces.

The civil war, which started in the province of Kenema in 1991, had not seriously impacted our lives in the city. Citizens in Freetown still enjoyed some element of peace in their normal daily life. Government services were running smoothly, and business was being conducted as usual. We occasionally heard news of the atrocities brewing in the countryside, in the bush, in the small rural villages, and in the diamond fields. Conflict over wealth in a poor country where diamonds litter the ground in alluvial fields, and workers hope for a cup of rice a day, threatened to take over all our lives.

News was increasingly more disturbing, and a large part of the country had been taken over by sadistic rebels. The chaotic situation was not encouraging, and getting worse. Graphic violence against civilians was shown on television, and no one understood why the rebels targeted innocent bystanders to maim, torture and kill: old men and women, young children, even infants.

The rebels' pattern of senseless violence was designed to instill terror in the citizens and the government, and to make it clear that if their demands for the nation's power and riches were not met, the whole country would suffer. Entering a poor village, they would line up every female to be raped and murdered; every man and child tortured and killed then leaves a select few alive to bear witness to their cruelty. Pregnant women were raped, cut open, their babies killed, and the women left to bleed to death.

On the open highway, vehicles were ambushed and passengers removed at gunpoint.

"Please don't kill me. Have mercy on me." Begging for their lives, the people would be forced to kneel and asked if they prefer short sleeve or long sleeve?

"We are not going to kill you; but you cannot come in contact with us, and we let you go like that. We must give you a mark that will remind you and tell people that you met us. So what do you want, short sleeve or long sleeve? Which one do you choose?"

Confused, people might stammer out short sleeve or long sleeve, one other, not knowing the rebels would hack off their arms with a machete at the wrist or the elbow. Short sleeve or long sleeve. Some were forced to make a choice between their leg or their arm-which one would they like to have cut of? And if they where to slow making their decision, the rebels would decide for them if they were not lucky, they were brutally murdered.

The rebels captured a man, his wife and five children in their home. With a dull blade they hacked off one of the man's legs and handed it to his wife, saying, "Here. Hold this for your husband." The man was yelling, screaming, and shouting in pain as they cut off his other leg and gave it to one of the children. "Here. Hold this for your father." The rebels told them not to cry, or they would shoot them. After this terrible act, they left the whole family in that state.

In the town of Kono, rebels killed every single person they saw and then burned their houses. The entire town of Kono was in flames.

In another town, rebels gathered everyone inside the hall of a large building, locked them in, and set the building on fire. Hundreds of people were burned alive. If they tried to escape, the rebels killed them as they ran out.

To this day, thousands of amputees have become the horrible life signature of the Sierra Leone rebels. Handicapped in this most gruesome manner, unable to walk or work or feed themselves, they bear the scars of their encounter with the devil, just as the Bible describes the antichrist's mark of the beast 666. It can never be erased.

This is how ruthless and wicked the rebels were. Led by Mr. Foday Sankoh, a first-class terrorist, a blood-soaked demon in human flesh with no mercy or regard for human life, they mobilized fighters by the thousands to join the cause of the RUF, Revolutionary United Front. I believed there was another force behind the rebels responsible for these heinous and unimaginable crimes. They must have been under a demonic force. The devil had arrived in Sierra Leone just to kill and destroy.

> *The thief cometh not, but for to steal, and to kill, and to destroy: I am come that they might have life, and that they might have [it] more abundantly (John 10:10).*

Nobody could stop the rebels. The Sierra Leone military and private security forces were short-handed, out-numbered, ineffective, and suspected by many of corruption and cooperation with the rebels. The world was not paying attention to this tiny, poor country on the coast of West Africa, and trying to bring peace to the escalating conflict seemed to be a losing battle.

Instead of leaving the country to conduct more evangelical crusades, I decided to stay and take a stand against the enemy. While the war was going on, I organized spiritual warfare prayer sessions to combat the evil of the rebels' action. We asked God for help, and believed in God's power to stand against these rebels and secure peace in our part of the country. Through fervent prayer, we asked God to uproot the rebels out of Sierra Leone and destroy every force of these rebellious demons.

Most of the time, we invited the military officers to join us in prayers. The man mobilizing the military officers, the late Mr. Tamba Mondel, was the spokesman for our ministry, the All Nations Gospel Outreach Ministries. He also happened to be the older brother of the Sierra Leone Army Chief of Staff. He had a very strong influence on the Sierra Leone government under President Captain Valentine Strasser, called the National Provisional Ruling Council. Because the new leaders could see that God was using me, they asked me to serve as spiritual advisor to the government. I served with this provisional government for the period of time they were in power, until they changed to a civilian government.

Spiritual warfare prayers were broadcast over the national radio, and Isaac Dennis became a household name. The rebel leaders knew my name from hearing my prayers on the radio in the bush, but they did not know my face.

This situation went on for some time and became worse and worse. The fighting was spreading in intensity and range, and the country was in terrible turmoil. The British, American, and Nigerian governments sent military experts to train the Sierra Leone military and recruit many youths into service. A contingent from the West African peacekeeping force called ECOMOG added strength and military expertise to the fray, and the International Red Cross and United Nations contributed diplomatic efforts on Sierra Leone's behalf. Finally, the world was aware of the problem and trying to help.

The rebels began to reach out to international sources for weapons and recruits to bolster their strength and numbers. They recruited by force and focused on children as young as six, impressionable and innocent, ready to be imprinted by the rebels' evil methods. Rebel bands would enter a household and kill everyone in it except the young boys, demanding that they enlist or be killed themselves. In some cases, the rebels killed one or two family members, then handed the weapon to the boy, commanding him to kill his own mother and father. If he refused, he was killed. If he complied, they would ask the boy to drink the blood of his parents as a form of initiation into the rebels' group.

These child soldiers became vicious mercenaries. With no compassion for people's lives, they would angrily say to someone begging for mercy, "I killed my mother and my father, and I drank their blood. Who are you not to be killed?" Their cruelty spread across the country, and led to more innocent children being recruited and initiated into this high level of witchcraft. A very evil spirit had invaded the country, bringing with it so much disaster; it had become a country of blood. Hearing and seeing all these things made my heart bleed; pain and sorrow filled my soul.

It was not that I had experienced personally any of these atrocities, nor my family nor my people, but as the spiritual leader of the nation, the people of Sierra Leone were my own people. They were my brothers and sisters, my mother and my father. I loved them so much because God had sent me to this country, and I had adopted the nation. I needed to stand and play my own part spiritually. Day and night, I was consumed with the question, "What can I do to save the people of Sierra Leone?"

In 1996, I organize a powerful Spiritual Warfare Conference for the armed forces of Sierra Leone. The purpose was to pray for the military. More than three dozen military personnel came to the conference to pray for God's intervention in the war and for God's protection for the soldiers. At the end of the meeting, a journalist interviewed me about what I expected God to do.

This was an opportunity to send a message to the rebels that they should give up killing people; this was not the will of God for their lives. The Bible forbids murder. I warned them that those who kill by the sword would also perish by the sword.

> *He that leadeth into captivity shall go into captivity: he that killeth with the sword must be killed with the sword. Here is the patience and the faith of the saints (Revelation 13:10).*

There was no secret on whose side I stood; it was clear I was against them and everything they stood for. The journalist put my picture in the newspaper, so now the rebels had my picture and I became a target: the preacher who spoke out against their cause.

Sometimes for twenty-one days at a time, my team and I would stay in prayer all night long. We prayed for God's intervention. Our greatest prayer was to stop the war, stop the killing, and stop the flow of blood.

One time, I was praying on my knees at midnight, and the Lord told me, "Isaac, I am sending you to the warfront."

"Lord, why are you sending me there?"

He told me He was sending me to pray for the Sierra Leone soldiers fighting on the warfront. I was so troubled.

"God, if you are sending me there, I commit my life to you. Whatever happens to me, my life is in Your hands; because if You send me there, You have a reason for this."

After praying, I called the military headquarters. I knew the chaplain was a believer, and I told him that the Lord was sending me to the warfront to pray for the soldiers. He asked where I would want to go.

"Kenema"

"Look, Evangelist Dennis, you are highly favored and recognized in this country. Are you sure you want to do that?" He told me Kenema was very dangerous; there was a lot of gunfire being exchange, and most people did not return alive.

"Put me on the next military truck with the soldiers who are going to Kenema." He asked me to think about it, but I told him I didn't need to. The Lord had already asked me to go.

A few days later, he called. A military truck was leaving that evening. I boarded with the soldiers. When we drove through Freetown, everything was peaceful, and there was no sign of war in the country. Upon arriving at Kenema, we started seeing houses that had been burned. Dead bodies littered the route. The whole area smelled of death. On the highway, we saw burned cards and buses with murdered passengers. The sight of it was painfully unreal and saddening.

As we drove, the soldiers told me that rebels often ambushed convoys and trucks on the road in order to stop soldiers from getting to their base. They also raided homes for food, killed the people, and burned the houses. I saw for the first time the aftermath of this rampage of violence and brutality all across the countryside.

As we got a bit further inside the frontline of the battlefield, we heard shooting. The rebels were attacking us. We were in an open truck, and the soldiers ordered me to lie down on the floor. Six of the soldiers stayed with me, while the others jumped out and fought back. The attack was over in about thirty minutes, and we unceremoniously continued our journey. The soldiers had overpowered the rebels, and thankfully, none of us were injured or killed. This was my first experience ever being in the midst of crossfire. I was shaken.

The rebels had retreated, but they were aware of our presence now, and this dangerous road was our only route. My eyes darted from one side of the road to the other, anticipating another attack. When we arrived at the military camp, the Captain was not happy to see an unarmed preacher brought into harm's way. The only civilian among two hundred soldiers, I stayed with them for four days, praying for them. Every morning I conducted prayers. During the parading, I stood in the midst of the soldiers and lifted up my Bible as they lifted up their arms. I released the Word of God upon them, and the Protection of God on their lives.

During these four days, there was peace in the surrounding area. The rebels did not attack any of the villages, which was in itself a miracle. The Captain informed me that during my stay there, the soldiers went into the bush and returned with no report of attacks. The rebels were there in the bush; but I believe that because God had sent me there at that moment, the Angel of God was with me.

When Daniel was cast in the lion's den, God send His Angel to shut the lion's mouth.

> *Then said Daniel unto the king, O king, live for ever. My God hath sent his angel, and hath shut the lions' mouths, that they have not hurt me: forasmuch as before him innocency was found in me; and also before thee, O king, have I done no hurt. Then was the king exceeding glad for him, and commanded that they should take Daniel up out of the den. So Daniel was taken up out of the den, and no manner of hurt was found upon him, because he believed in his God. And the king commanded, and they brought those men which had accused Daniel, and they cast [them] into the den of lions, them,*

*their children, and their wives; and the lions
had the mastery of them, and brake all their
bones in pieces or ever they came at the bottom
of the den (Daniel 6:21-24).*

The rebels were quiet because of God's anointing. Almost all the soldiers there professed Jesus Christ as their Lord and Savior. They were very open to my ministry, because they needed the protection of God from the daily dangers that beset their lives. It was a perilous but successful mission.

I returned to Freetown to continue my crusade against the war. The Captain requested my return, but my mission was only for that one trip. Some of the soldiers visited me in appreciation for my support when they came back to Freetown, and I was glad for any small part I could play in keeping them safe.

Matinda, a woman from my church in Freetown, was proud of her son who had left school at the age of nineteen to join the military in defense of his country. A recipient of the Medal of Honor, he showed courage in battle and was known by the nickname "RPG Launcher" because of his skill with the weapon. Before he left for the warfront, I called him and said a special prayer for God's protection. He left with his troop. After a fierce fight with only one battalion of soldiers against hundreds of rebels, he alone managed to escape alive. Every other member of his team died.

Matinda testified, "My son explained how the battle went. He said, 'Mama, the God of Pastor Dennis is real. He prayed for me before I left and gave me a pocket Bible. I put it in the chest pocket of my uniform. The bullet that should have killed me hit this Bible.' He took the Bible out and showed me the bullet."

God answered our prayers with the Bible as a shield, confirming the belief that if God wants to save someone's life, He can use anything to do it. Matinda's son became a living testimony to the power of prayer, and advised everyone around him, "Before you go to the warfront, go and meet Pastor Dennis and get him to pray for you."

Before long, that is exactly what happened. Many soldiers came for prayers of protection before leaving for battle. Sometimes, God would inspire me to forbid a soldier from going, because they would not come back alive. My spokesman's brother, the Army Chief of Staff, Captain Komba Mondel wanted to go to the warfront to see how the armed forces were doing and to encourage them. I knew nothing of these plans, but one afternoon when I was saying my prayers, the Lord revealed to me that I should call my friend and tell his brother to stop every plan he was making. I made the phone call. I talked with my friend and asked him about his brother. He told me his brother was already on his way. I asked if there was any way to radio him to turn back immediately. I told him that if there was, he should. If not, his brother would not come back alive. These people took my words very seriously, because they had witnessed how the Lord was revealing prophecy through me. When my friend heard this advice, he radioed his brother from military headquarters, and was told that he was already close to the front line. The message from Pastor Dennis was relayed, and the command quickly given to stop the convoy. The Chief of Staff returned with some of his security staff, while the rest of the convoy continued to the battlefront. Before he arrived in Freetown, my friend's brother received news that everyone in the convoy had died. He lost most of his top security men in that rebel attack.

The rebels of the RUF had by this time identified me by the picture that was published in the newspaper, and my full involvement as a spiritual warfare leader had earned my name a place on the list of enemies they wanted to kill in Freetown. And they were closing in. The city of Freetown is a peninsula with only one exit by land, through Waterloo, which the rebels had already taken. Millions of people were trapped in Freetown with no escape except by sea, a route many people tried to take by boat. News on the radio and television announced repeatedly that the rebels had blocked the major exit out of the city and were marching to Freetown.

Fear, panic, and despair filled the hearts of the millions living in the city, including hundreds of foreigners. The only thing the people of Freetown could do was pray. A strong sense of unity pushed aside religious differences, and people of all faiths began to beseech God for rescue. At this point, it seemed to me everyone believed only the name of Jesus Christ could save them from the impending terror. Even some Muslims in Freetown began to pray to God in the name of Jesus. If the rebels entered Freetown, no one would be safe. They were ready to kill and destroy without mercy.

Intelligence reports estimated that sixteen thousand rebels surrounded Freetown and were ready to march in and attack.

People wealthy enough to fly by helicopter from the city were fleeing to the airport in Lungi, where the Nigerian army had set up a base. Everyone else waited, and prayed. We had been assured that the ECOWAS peacekeeping force and the Nigerian army were there to protect the whole city. However, unknown to the public, the peacekeeping forces and the Nigerian soldiers had pulled out, leaving the city open to attack from the rebels.

Early one morning, to our surprise and dismay, the media announced that sixteen thousand armed rebels had entered Freetown, and advised all civilians to stay indoors. We felt deserted and exposed. We later learned that the soldiers removed their military uniforms and put on civilian clothes to blend with the crowd, giving them a chance to regroup. The rebels met no open resistance, and thought they had gained victory. The year was 1997.

CHAPTER NINE
HOTEL MAMMY YOKO

CHAPTER NINE
Hotel Mammy Yoko

The announcement on the radio said that every foreigner should take refuge in the Mammy Yoko Hotel. I was taking my usual afternoon rest at my home, a time I had set apart as my quiet time where I communed with God, and therefore did not allow anyone to knock on my door or disturb me. My old friend, Mr. Gideon, came to my house with a driver sent by the Nigerian Ambassador. They were told I was resting and could not be disturbed. They left a message urging me to go to the Nigerian Embassy as soon as possible. I overheard their conversation, but did not come out from my room. After they left, I asked what was going on. They told me the Nigerian Ambassador had sent his car to pick me up because of the threats of the rebels. I had no relationship with the Nigerian Ambassador. It struck me as odd that he sent his car to pick me up. Something was not right. I told everyone to get ready and follow me.

We went to the church, and I asked them to stay while I found out what was going on. At the Embassy gate a guard said, "Hey, stop there." I gave him my name. He asked if I was the preacher, and I answered in the affirmative. He grabbed me and pushed me quickly towards the entrance. He said I was very lucky to have arrived there at that time, because the rebels were on their way to my home.

The soldiers asked if I had left any people in the house. He was relieved to hear that I had taken everyone to the church. He told me the only place I could go was the Mammy Yoko Hotel, where all foreigners were taking refuge. As a matter of fact, he went on, the Nigerian Ambassador was already there and had received word of my safe location. A few minutes after my arrival at the Embassy, a message arrived that the rebels had entered my home and shooting the entire building down, expecting me of hiding on the roof. When they found nothing, they moved on. The Nigerian Embassy was obviously monitoring the movement of the rebels and was well informed of their activities.

From inside the car, I peered out into the streets of Freetown. This was the city I had walked freely, and whose people had become like my own dear family. The memories of my experiences there were suddenly so near, and yet at once so foreign. Like a stranger, I was being escorted at risk of my life into a secure place of refuge. At the gate of the Mammy Yoko Hotel, Nigerian soldiers guarded the entrance against invaders and local civilians, allowing only foreigners with proper identification to pass inside. Joining the large throng of Nigerians, Ghanaians, Europeans, British, Americans, and Lebanese, we felt safe under the protection of a battalion of thirty men stationed there.

The manager of the hotel provided haven and food for a growing crowd of refugees, far outnumbering the rooms available. People slept in the lobby and conference rooms while awaiting evacuation, and quickly made acquaintance with the odd community of new and old friends sharing a common bond in time of trial.

British paratroopers were the first to arrive and take most of the European citizens to safety. A few days later, long buses took American citizens to the beach, where they were transported by helicopter to an American gunship at sea. Two days later, Lebanese citizens were shipped to the neighboring country of Sierra Leone, Guinea. Those of us left behind, some five hundred foreigners mostly from African countries, felt our hopes of rescue dwindling each day. We heard no plans for any further evacuations, so we listened to the news and waited.

People sat together in groups, drinking and smoking. Some listened to their music players, danced, played games, talked, or walked the halls of the hotel to pass the time. I began leading prayers each day from 4:00 a.m. to 6:00 a.m.

Outside, all manner of atrocities continued in Freetown, the city of terror. The government had fled, leaving one rebel Mr. Johnny Paul Koroma of the RUF as the self-proclaimed President of Sierra Leone. As his legacy, the order of the day was to continue the brutal dismemberment of innocent citizens at the whim of sadistic rebel soldiers on the rampage. Homes were raided and ransacked, women and girls raped, and hands amputated. People were called out, gunned down, and chopped in pieces. We watched the news in horror and thanked God we were under protection of armed soldiers.

Sleeping on crowded floors, we took every opportunity to spend time in the hotel's rear courtyard, finding ways to pass the time. One sunny afternoon, a young rebel boy suddenly appeared in our midst brandishing a rifle. He lifted his gun and opened fire into the air, shocking us into the realization that we were not as safe as we thought. How had he penetrated the protective hotel perimeter of thirty soldiers? There in the courtyard, the young boy held more than three hundred people at gunpoint. Soldiers rushed in when they heard the gunshot, but held back for fear of antagonizing the boy into firing on us. We all held our breath. The rebel's boy screamed at everyone to stay back, threatening to shoot us all if anyone tried to stop him.

A man from my church, Chief Moudagar, moved closer to the boy. In his fifties, he took a fatherly tone and tried to placate the young rebel with soothing words.

"Young man, look. You are a very handsome boy. I could be a father to you, and I know that you do not mean what you are doing right now. Maybe you want food. You can tell us. We are ready to give it to you. If you open fire and shoot these innocent people, it will not do you any good. Put down your gun, and we can give you some food."

Eventually, the boy put down his weapon and left. He did not need anything except information to report back to the rebels regarding the size and strength of the battalion of soldiers guarding the hotel. It was only a matter of time before we too would be under attack, and the soldiers prepared for battle. One told me, "Pastor, you have to start praying. That rebel boy came in here to spy, so there is going to be an attack."

Quietness is my reclusion. I desperately needed some now, with time to think and pray. Hundreds of people were singing, dancing, talking, and eating - oblivious to the impending danger. That evening before we went to sleep, I called everybody together for prayers. Early the next morning, May 29, 1997 at 4:00 a.m., we all came together again for prayers. From outside the front gates, our large group of people was visible spilling from the lobby and conference rooms. We stood together to pray for peace, security and safety, for strength to face our enemies; we prayed for our families and loved ones, the city, the war-torn country, and for the world.

After about thirty minutes, I asked the people to sit down, so we could read the Bible. There in the midst of them, I alone remained on my feet. Despite our prayers, the unthinkable happened. At 5:00 a.m. we heard an explosion on the fourth floor and felt the vibration shake the whole building. The rebels launched a shell into one of the rooms, and the room caught on fire. We were under attack. A soldier rushed in and shouted, "Everybody down!" as bullets ripped through the windows and walls of the conference room, pinning everyone to the floor and scattering broken glass over the top of them. In shock, I stood holding my Bible until a young man jumped on me and pulled me to the floor. For the next two hours, people screamed and cried under heavy fire.

By 7:00 a.m. the soldiers had succeeded in pushing the rebels back, and they asked the hotel manager if there was a more secure place to put us, because the rebels were bent on killing everybody. He opened the basement and led us below ground to a smaller room. We crowded together, over five hundred of us.

"How many rebels are there?" someone asked, and one soldier estimated about two hundred, maybe more.

"And how many soldiers are here?" came the question.

"Thirty."

The Captain came to the basement himself. "We will give our lives to save you," he assured us. "The only way the rebels can get to you is if all thirty of us are dead."

From the basement room we listened as the fighting continued overhead. There was no ventilation, no food or water, and many people fainted from heat and dehydration. The temperature reached 32° C (90° F) that afternoon in the basement, and although there were two nurses among us who administrated first aid, what we needed most was water. Sounds of battle raged above us: people screaming in different languages, bullets, footsteps running, explosions, breaking glass, and crashing pieces of the hotel. Sometimes the building shook so hard we thought it would collapse and bury us all alive. No one dared leave the basement to retrieve water for the unconscious; but there was one boy who was brave enough to go up and get water for the people who were fainting, mostly women and children.

At one point the soldiers came inside carrying one from their battalion who had been shot in the leg. Now there were twenty-nine soldiers remaining to protect us. News of the battle was encouraging, the wounded soldier said, as they had killed many of the rebels already. The soldiers were better trained, better equipped, and had heavier weapons than the rebels. Above all, though, I believe we were under the protection of God, but they were seriously outnumbered and knew that more rebels were on the way. The soldiers were as determined to hold their position as the rebels were to enter the hotel.

By then the small basement had become so messy and overwhelmed with heat, crying, screaming, and unconscious people that nerves strained to the breaking point. One man grabbed me by the neck and pushed me to the wall, shouting, "Pastor Dennis, why do you leave us here to die?"

"I am not God! I cannot stop the rebels."

Another man begged, "Pastor, Pastor, pray for us." His voice was joined by others, "Please, Pastor, please Pastor, pray for us."

Their please tore me apart, and I realized they were ready to trust God. My question to them needed to be answered: "Do you all believe that if we pray, God will deliver us?"

"Yes! Yes! Yes!" everybody shouted.

Hope and refuge came to me from the words of the Holy Scripture:

And call upon me in the day of trouble: I will deliver thee, and thou shalt glorify me (Psalms 50:15).

We all prayed for God to deliver us. As I led the prayer, everybody shouted, "Amen!" the soldiers fought outside while we prayed inside, down in the basement. The British reporter, Elizabeth Blond, reported the battle as it ensued at the Mammy Yoko Hotel, and people all over Africa listening to *Voice of Africa* on BBC Radio heard developments of the fighting as it was reported. Five soldiers were wounded and brought to the basement, and with each casualty we counted down the remaining battalion protecting the hotel: we were down to twenty-five against many time more rebels.

At about 6:00 p.m., the International Red Cross negotiated a peace agreement with RUF leaders, including and order to cease fire at the Mammy Yoko Hotel. Suddenly all the fighting stopped. We didn't know what the quiet above our heads meant. We sat and stood in silent expectation waiting to see who would open the door, friend or foe. The door opened and soldiers came down to tell us the battle was over. Everybody rejoiced and praised God for His deliverance.

As we emerged from the basement, we looked around in the fading light of sunset at the devastation of the city. Bodies of about a hundred rebels killed in battle lay in the streets where they fell. According to the soldiers, many more were on their way to join them when the ceasefire was called.

One soldier told me, "We believe that it was God who intervened and gave us the strength; if not, we would not have been able to overcome the rebels." We thanked God for preserving us that day. No soldiers died, and everyone at Mammy Yoko Hotel emerged alive. This was the miracle of God's protection.

One of the conditions of the ceasefire was to relinquish the Mammy Yoko Hotel to the rebel leaders, where they planned to set up their own base. Another condition was for all foreigners to leave the city immediately, but we had nowhere to go. We dispersed into the surrounding area in the gathering twilight, looking for a tree, a bush, the beach, anywhere to sleep and take refuge. We were afraid and uncertain about what would happen next, and the majority of us were awake all night. I spent the night in prayer to God, asking Him to send us help in our hour of need.

Around 8:00 a.m. the sound of approaching helicopters sliced through the morning air. The helicopters were arriving from the west, the direction of the open sea, and two jets were also flying around. With panic striking our hearts, everyone ran helter skater looking for refuge, thinking the war had resumed. In the midst of the confusion, a helicopter landed on the beach and dispatched an armored car from the hold. White soldiers climbed out, then more helicopters, more armored cars, and more white soldiers. We asked each other what could be going on, and since no one had the answer, we continued to watch in fear.

The soldiers blocked the road with heavy barbed wire, creating a secure territory for themselves. The helicopters lifted off in the west and returned from the seas carrying hundreds of soldiers. We watched as they occupied the whole area, but we still didn't know who they were or why they were there. We hid in the bush and dared not to go near them, fearing the worst. After some time, one of the soldiers came to us with a heavy gun in his hand, a gun so big that it could not compare to the ones we had seen before. He announced that they were the U.S. Marines, and they had come to evacuate the people from the Mammy Yoko Hotel. Tears filled our eyes at the miracle of our delivery. Help had finally come! Everyone started jumping, running out of the bush from every corner, and shouting, "Thank God for America! Thank God for America!"

Soon, the evacuation was underway and lasted the whole day. People lined up to enter the helicopters and were given earphones for the trip over the high seas to the warship Kearsarge. The U.S. Marines evacuated not only the foreigners from the Mammy Yoko Hotel, but also anybody else who was willing to leave the country for safety. Over two thousand men, women, and children were flown to safety that day and housed on the Kearsarge. The U.S. Marines provided food and beds, made us comfortable, and treated us very well. With the hospitality we received, we didn't want to get off the ship! Everyone said, "Take us to America," even though we knew that was not possible.

The Captain came and announced that his ship was not going to America, but was stationed in the Mediterranean Sea, off the coast of Africa. After two days and one night aboard the Kearsarge, we were airlifted to Conakry in the Federal Republic of Guinea. Once we landed, I found a friend in Guinea who took me in.

Now with time to reflect on the events of my life in Sierra Leone, I realized God is so great. He is a very Big God who is always there when He is needed and invited. He answers prayers. The Bible says He will never leave His people, nor forsake them.

There shall not any man be able to stand before thee all the days of thy life: as I was with Moses, [so] I will be with thee: I will not fail thee, nor forsake thee (Joshua 1: 5).

In a situation where it seemed there was no way out, God was there to make a way. I recounted the reasons for my secure knowledge of the proof of God's existence. Many times in many ways I had witnessed God's manifestation in my life. The Bible says only a fool says there is no God.

To the chief Musician, [A Psalm] of David. The fool hath said in his heart, [There is] no God. They are corrupt, they have done abominable works, [there is] none that doeth good (Psalm 14: 1).

In everything I had been through—rejection, frustration, cold, hunger, sickness, gunfire, and death threats—God's help gave me the strength to make it through and prevail through His goodness and mercy. I always felt His presence by my side, and He continued to do great things in my life. I had learned to look up to God for help in the time of need and trouble:

I will lift up mine eyes unto the hills, from whence cometh my help. My help [cometh] from the LORD, which made heaven and earth. He will not suffer thy foot to be moved: he that keepeth thee will not slumber (Psalms 121:1-3).

I didn't want to make the mistake many people make, looking for help from the wrong source. That would be like taking a broken car to a shoemaker instead of a mechanic. Shoes are the shoemaker's specialty, not cars. It is the same in spiritual matters. God is the One who made us. He alone can fix us when we are broken. He knows what to do because He knows what He put in us; and therefore, He is the Source of our help and healing.

And God said, Let us make man in our image, after our likeness: and let them have dominion over the fish of the sea, and over the fowl of the air, and over the cattle, and over all the earth, and over every creeping thing that creepeth upon the earth. So God created man in his [own] image, in the image of God created he him; male and female created he them. And God blessed them, and God said unto them, Be fruitful, and multiply, and replenish the earth, and subdue it: and have dominion over the fish of the sea, and over the fowl of the air, and over every living thing that moveth upon the earth (Genesis 1:26-28).

In the basement of the Mammy Yoko Hotel, I told the hundreds of people that the rebels did not give us life; therefore, they could not take it away. You can only take what belongs to you. If you take that which does not belong to you, it is stealing. Our lives belong to God. No one can steal them unless we allow it. The Lord protected us because we are the sheep of His pasture. He was with us in the basement just as He had been with me in every move I made and every step I took up to that point.

Shadrach, Meshach, and Abednego were put into the fiery furnace, a fire so hot that the flames even killed the men who put them inside.

> *And he commanded the most mighty men that [were] in his army to bind Shadrach, Meshach, and Abednego, [and] to cast [them] into the burning fiery furnace. 21 Then these men were bound in their coats, their hosen, and their hats, and their other garments, and were cast into the midst of the burning fiery furnace.*

> *22 Therefore because the king's commandment was urgent, and the furnace exceeding hot, the flame of the fire slew those men that took up Shadrach, Meshach, and Abednego.*

> *23 And these three men, Shadrach, Meshach, and Abednego, fell down bound into the midst of the burning fiery furnace.*

117

24 Then Nebuchadnezzar the king was astonied, and rose up in haste, and spake, and said unto his counsellors, Did not we cast three men bound into the midst of the fire? They answered and said unto the king, True, O king.

25 He answered and said, Lo, I see four men loose, walking in the midst of the fire, and they have no hurt; and the form of the fourth is like the Son of God.

26 Then Nebuchadnezzar came near to the mouth of the burning fiery furnace, and spake, and said, Shadrach, Meshach, and Abednego, ye servants of the most high God, come forth, and come hither. Then Shadrach, Meshach, and Abednego, came forth of the midst of the fire.

27 And the princes, governors, and captains, and the king's counsellors, being gathered together, saw these men, upon whose bodies the fire had no power, nor was an hair of their head singed, neither were their coats changed, nor the smell of fire had passed on them.

28 Then Nebuchadnezzar spake, and said, Blessed be the God of Shadrach, Meshach, and Abednego, who hath sent his angel, and delivered his servants that trusted in him, and have changed the king's word, and yielded their bodies, that they might not serve nor worship any god, except their own God (Daniel 3:20-28).

The fire did not burn them. The Lord turned the heat of the fire into air conditioning when He arrived in the midst as the Fourth Man. When facing hardship we may feel alone, but with a firm belief in God there is always a Second Person at our side.

Although safe from harm and delivered from danger, I needed to start my life all over again. Everything I build in Sierra Leone was lost in the devastation of the civil war. It was to be a new beginning.

CHAPTER TEN
REACHING THE GOAL

CHAPTER TEN
REACHING THE GOAL

The Isaac Dennis who arrived in Guinea was no longer the same young man, whom needs to start all over again from living in a junkyard car. Though, I left Freetown the same way I arrived, with only the suit I was wearing. My stature as spiritual advisor to the people of Sierra Leone, the military, and the leaders of the nation had elevated my position to one of recognition and respect. In worldly possessions, however, from humble beginning to total fulfillment to disaster, following God's path had been an eventful journey. As long as I had life, there was still hope and more than a million ways to explore. I needed to spend quality time in thought and prayer to ponder my options.

It would be easy to give up hope. This has become a common phenomenon in the world today, because people cannot face difficult challenges without grumbling. But the challenges of life constitute the most interesting part of life. Without tests of our faith, we cannot develop a testimony.

Vision kept me going, and that, in essence, is the purpose of each of our lives. My vision to reach the whole world with the Gospel of Jesus Christ was then and still is my life's goal. I refused to be stopped by any circumstances.

My ministry in Sierra Leone had become prosperous, and I was convinced that the same God who opened doors for me in Freetown would answer my knock in a new land. Although I arrived in the country of Guinea without any possessions, the Lord had blessed the work of my hands. The fame surrounding my name in Sierra Leone had also spread to Conakry, and this made it easier for me to have a breakthrough immediately.

People in Conakry learned of my presence and began coming to me, and soon churches were inviting me to speak. The hardships I went through in Sierra Leone were a thing of the past. Within nine months of my arrival in Guinea, I conducted a citywide Gospel Crusade through the help and support of the people I met there. The response was tremendous, with many miracles. The deaf heard; the mute spoke; the lame walked. This gathering was the second miracle crusade in the city's history, and I soon became known as the miracle evangelist. I established the first evangelistic outreach in Guinea. Everything that happened to me became an opportunity to make history. I found myself going where I was not known, without money or any form of support, but strong enough in faith to alter the course of events in the name of the Lord. Knowing that many will come to follow my footsteps as they see how God honors my faith in Him. This was a humbling responsibility, one that required consideration and prayer for direction.

God told me He wanted to use me in Europe. For any African, a visa to a European country is difficult to obtain. But I knew that if God called me and sent me to a place. He would open the door. God gave me the European vision; now it was up to me to prepare for it. In any new venture, whether business or personal, we may be faced with imposing obstacles. There are always a million reasons to doubt our hope for success. Failures stare us boldly in the face, but seeing beyond these distractions is where victory lies. I considered the chances of an African traveling to Europe. Without any contacts or invitations from close European friends, the task was made a thousand times more difficult.

The Bible says the earth and all its fullness is the Lord's.

> *The earth [is] the LORD'S, and the fulness thereof; the world, and they that dwell therein. For he hath founded it upon the seas, and established it upon the floods (Psalms 24:1-2).*

The Lord made the earth; He owns everything in it; and He can override rules and regulations made by men. Time and again I had witnessed this principle, so I took the first step of faith and went to the French Embassy, the British Embassy, and the Belgian Embassy. Each in turn denied me. Clearly there was no compelling reason to grant me permission to go to their country. But the Bible says that with men this things are impossible, but with God all things are possible.

> *And he said, The things which are impossible with men are possible with God (Luke 18:27).*

125

Even visa rejections did not deter me. Somehow the barriers to my European mission could be crossed, through legal means. I knew I will not need to act like Mission Impossible, part 1, 2 and 3 before it becomes possible.

I can do all things through Christ which strengtheneth me (Philippians 4:13).

I puzzled, "How do I get there?"

In the face of insurmountable obstacles, it helps to have someone to encourage us. Our role models can influence us to push forward, make it happen, and never give up. Watching and copying the practices of successful businessmen, preachers, teachers, parents, athletes, and leaders is a good way to realize our own potential. There is a lot of potential sleeping in the graveyard. I knew I did not want to go to my grave with my potential. I want to be counted among the noble men and women who have changed the world and made history; like Bill Gates a successful businessmen, a powerful preacher like Billy Graham in America and a television show host, Oprah Winfrey.

My friends and contacts rallied around to help me. I felt blessed to have come so far from the lonely days in Freetown when I had no one to call "Brother." If you ask most people in prison how they got there, they will tell you a story beginning with "I had a friend." If you have friends who do not create positive impact in your life, disconnect from them. If you are pursuing a vision that will not benefit you, quit. Choose the class of people who bolster your confidence and your aspirations. My friends have influenced me for success and blessed me with their comfort and support in achieving my goals.

Unfortunately it was not my desire to settle permanently in Guinea, I needed to hand over the ministry to my very dear friend and son in the Lord, Pastor Felix Robert. Then with a plane ticket to leave Africa, I traveled first to Moscow for a weekend, then to Cuba with the intention of breaking the Fidel Castro Gospel barrier. My plan was to organize a city-wide crusade in Havana, Cuba, but after a weekend there I flew to the Bahamas. It was my first time to leave Africa, and it felt like a world tour. The question of how to make a change in people's lives consumed my thoughts.

After a short stay, I prepared to leave the Bahamas. At the airport an immigration officer asked me where I was going.

"I don't know. I don't have a ticket to any destination. I came into the Bahamas with a one-way ticket."

"Where is your return ticket?" he asked.

"I have none."

"How is it possible for you to come to the Bahamas without a return ticket? You have no intention of leaving the Bahamas!" he accused angrily.

A quiet prayer for direction was my only reply for a few moments. I knew God was going to use me in Europe. "I want to go to France."

"There is a flight boarding for Paris now. May I see your passport, please?"

He directed the airline to check in my luggage and gave my passport to the pilot for the French police.

My name was not on the manifest; I didn't buy a ticket; I didn't have a visa; but I was on the flight with a good seat like anybody else. When we arrived in France, the French police asked to see my visa.

"I don't have one."

"Do you know that you cannot enter France without a visa?"

"I know that, but when I went to the French embassy in Nigeria, I was refused one."

Curiously, they studied the situation. "Then how did you get on the flight from the Bahamas to Paris without a ticket and visa?"

"Miracles still happen. I am walking on God's Miracle. God told me to preach in France."

They looked at me in surprise. I could understand the French phrase one officer said to the other, "This man is complicated. Let us send him back to the Bahamas."

"Ça ce n'est pas possible," I replied. ("That is not possible.")

They discussed my confusing case until I interjected, "I can help you make a decision. I have traveled on a fourteen-hour flight to get here. I am tired, and I need a place to rest."

They arranged for me to stay at the five-star Ibis Hotel under police guard; then the next morning brought me back to the airport.

"We have arranged your flight back to the Bahamas," they reported.

"Paris is my destination, and I am not traveling any longer."

For four days the Ibis Hotel provided me with very fine VIP treatment while authorities deliberated my case. On December 9, 1999 legal procedures were completed admitting me into France. It was freezing. I may have been used to tropical temperatures, but God's promise to take me to impossible places had been fulfilled.

January 2000 witnessed the beginning of my European Outreach Ministry in the new millennium. I preached in a church in Germany for two weeks. When I returned to Paris, the Lord directed me to travel to Belgium. By now I was used to going to foreign countries without any contact. I arrived at Brussels Midi train station and looked for an inexpensive hotel. Two African boys in the street nearby looked friendly.

'Where can I find a hotel for under $50?"

One boy, Steve, asked two questions in return. "Why are you looking for a hotel?

And what are you doing in Brussels?"

"I am a preacher. The Lord sent me here to preach."

"Who is your contact in Brussels?" he continued.

"I have none, except you that I just met."

"Because you are a man of God, I am going to show you my house," said Steve. "If you don't like it, I can take you to a hotel."

Steve's house was a very nice bachelor studio, and he invited me to stay there. That Saturday evening Steve took me to his church. No one was there. As we left, I met Pastor Tony Silasi and his secretary, Antonia. Through his secretary as interpreter, he invited me to come preach in his church the next day. I was puzzled. I had only given him my name. The fact that I was a preacher was never mentioned. I declined his invitation and decided not to go.

The next afternoon as I lay resting, I heard the Lord calling me, "Isaac, stand up and go to that church." Naturally, I obeyed.

It was 5:00 p.m. when I slipped into a back pew, two hours late for the service. No one would notice me. The congregation of 400 black Africans was a pretty sure bet for me to blend in. However, somebody notified the Pastor that maybe the man in the back row was the man he had been waiting for.

In French, Pastor Tony asked me to come forward. He told the congregation that he didn't know how to introduce me. He could not remember my name, since he had only met me yesterday. We did not speak the same language as one another. But Pastor Tony heard God tell him that I was a man of God. Upon this fact, he had invited me to come and preach. This convinced me that God opens doors to accomplish His purpose.

I took the microphone and introduced myself. Meeting this pastor by surprise, without anybody's introduction, was a divine connection. This example served to encourage those present to take the step of faith in obedience to God, and the Lord would not disappoint them, as He had not disappointed me. God is the Introducer.

I ministered to the congregation in a powerful service. God presented me to the people by releasing an indescribable anointing upon the church. I was surprised to see the kind of great manifestation that took place that day in Belgium. I was invited back, and the next time I preached there, the hall could not contain the number of people who had gathered to hear me.

After ministering in that church for a couple of months, the Lord sent me to the city of Kortrijk, West Flanders. There it was rare to see a black man on the street, and the color difference was an obstacle to making friends. Belgium is the most difficult place I have ever been to preach the gospel. Not all the people of Belgium dislike blacks, but persecution is a fact of life there.

A beautiful lady from Pastor Tony's church in Brussels had begun to help me translate correspondence and coordinate my ministry around the country. Christa became a wonderful instrument for good in my life, and we developed a strong working relationship. As we became more connected in our common cause, it was not easy to avoid falling in love. We married and started a family. A great spouse can make such a difference in the life of a man. Christa's support and love ignited a dramatic change. She saw through my toughness to the real me inside. In spite of my idiosyncrasies, she applied her balm of love and tender care, and smoothed many of the rough edges of my life.

Starting the church in Kortrijk was a great challenge, because people there considered themselves superior to me. They needed me to prove myself to them as honest and sincere before they eventually became receptive. It took six months to establish our Flemish church of close to 150 white members, only five black Africans, and the only black pastor I knew of in the city.

Other Flemish pastors became jealous and began to persecute us. Most of them had ministered for ten or twenty years with a congregation of twenty members or less. The large congregations attending our healing revival services were gathering from all across Belgium. We began allowing people to travel the day before and sleep in the church to attend services the following day. The Healing Ministry was so powerful that people even came in wheelchairs and went back home walking. Spiritual lives were revived. The Holy Spirit moved in another dimension.

Some pastors went on the offensive to fight the fellowship of our church. The spread false rumors, which led to a police investigation of our so-called miracles. We broke no laws. Our church meetings continued. Police officers would sometimes walk in during a service, but the unseen presence of God stopped them from taking any action.

The faith of our church congregation was stronger than ever. We drew up plans to build the first Pentecostal Cathedral in Kortrijk, West Flanders, Belgium.

Other pastors warned me against the power of darkness in the city. Ministers before me had faced demonic forces and folded within three months. Our church was no exception. Negative spiritual forces frequently attacked us, even during church service when I was preaching the Gospel. The Bible tells of forces of darkness, territorial demons, princesses and queens of darkness.

> *For we wrestle not against flesh and blood, but against principalities, against powers, against the rulers of the darkness of this world, against spiritual wickedness in high [places] (Ephesians 6:12).*

These spirits can take control over people's affairs and manipulate their minds to do despicable things. They can also cause people to reject the influence of the Holy Spirit and spread dissention and contention around them.

In order to penetrate these zones, it is important to know that God is the one leading you there. Not every preacher understands how to stand against the forces of darkness. In

Africa, voodoos are tied around the body so that the demon appears very fearful and deadly. With African voodoo, one can see right away you are dealing with witchcraft. European witchcraft is practiced in a more subtle way. There is no physical sign of voodoo. It is carried in the spirit, and there is no way it can be discerned except by listening to the Spirit of God. After a few months, God began to reveal the dark spirits who operated under the pretense of being church members. They started manifesting their true nature.

CHAPTER ELEVEN
OPEN CHALLENGE

CHAPTER ELEVEN
OPEN CHALLENGE

Christa and I opened our office to counsel people. We received a man who had made an appointment for counseling, claiming to be in need of prayers. Actually, he had plans to challenge me in order to find out how powerful I was. As a man I am not powerful; but with the Spirit of God giving me strength, I am greater than a giant.

He told me he had tested every pastor in every church in West Flanders. None of them had any power over him. They all prayed for him and nothing happened. He told me the Spirit forces that control the city of Kortrijk were in him. So if I prayed for him, nothing would happen. He kept on telling me that he was very powerful and no amount of prayers could do anything to him. I was ready to walk him out of my office. He probably thought I was a noisemaker. On second thought, he might tell his colleagues he had challenged me and nothing had happened. I decided to show him a little bit of the power of God.

I asked him if he was there to test how powerful I was, as he had tried with the other pastors. I asked him to stand and lift up his hands, as he had done with the other pastors. I commanded the spirit in him to leave in the name of Jesus Christ. In less than a minute, he fell down manifesting different kinds of animals. He spread out like a crab, then a dog, then his eyes became as a cat. The prayer lasted just about ten minutes. When I stopped, I asked what he thought. He couldn't say anything. He left and never came back.

In August 2001, we made plans to conduct the first open air crusade in the history of Flanders. For thirty days, our congregation fasted and prayed for the government to give us the necessary permit. It was granted. Our crusade was announced.

Two weeks before the crusade, the witches cause it to rain. The rain fell copiously while the advertisement for the crusade played on Flemish television WTV. Everyone grumbled and complained about the unpredictability of the European weather. Why would Isaac Dennis put a crusade outdoors without a tent? All my church members were discouraged. They worried I had led them to open shame.

Europeans hate failure. They want everything to be perfect. Fear of failure can prevent success. My philosophy is to fail once, fail twice, or fail as many times as it takes, but never stop trying. The past does not dictate the future. My attitude is to keep trying until I score the goal.

God answered my prayer. He told me I should not be worried: the day the crusade begins, the rain will stop; the day the crusade ends, the rain will start again.

I went to the church to announce to the discouraged congregation what the Lord had told me. Their faces told me they didn't believe me. Maybe they thought I was a comedian trying to cover my mistake. "What is this man saying? Is he joking or what?" The situation looked impossible by any rational standard. For me, however, reason and logic had nothing to do with it. I knew in whom I believed. The Creator could manage even the weather. My optimism drove us forward.

And indeed, according to the Word of God, the rain stopped before 3:00 a.m. the day of the crusade. In spite of weather forecasts for continued rain, at 7:00 a.m. the beautiful sun appeared and raised the temperature over 32∘C (90∘F). Everybody was astounded.

The hot weather lasted four days while we conducted the open-air crusade. People came to ask, "Pastor Dennis, can you please ask your God to give us some more days of good weather, so we can go to the beach?"

"No, there is no extension. The rain is going to start falling."

The leader of occult forces in the city of Kortrijk was very popular and greatly feared. On the fourth day of the crusade, he attended the prayer meeting to challenge me face-to-face. His mission was to accuse me of trying to take the city from his hands, and to tell me I had neither right nor power to do so. He claimed to control the city. I told him that night's events would determine who had power and ownership of the city, him or God.

I went on stage and told everybody in the crusade to stand up and pray.

"Lift up your hands to the sky," I asked them. Then I prayed, "I release the Fire of God to come down upon the city of Kortrijk. Let the Holy Ghost Fire begin to consume every occult witch and wizard."

No forces of darkness could escape the Judgment of God. I asked God to release this very powerful fire prayer upon the city of Kortrijk. We did our prayer by faith and waited for God to give us the result.

The crusade ended at 11:00 p.m. August 25, 2001. As our team left the crusade ground in a truck filled with equipment, the heavy rain resumed. That was an obvious miracle. Soon, I gained the reputation as a man who stopped the rain. However, I attributed it to the One who granted our prayers: God.

At about midnight that night, we received a phone call from the wife of the occult leader. She did not know what was going on with her husband. He was screaming about seeing fire tormenting him, and he needed help. She asked if I could come pray for him that night. This was the man who had just told me that he was the prince of Kortrijk, and the power of the city was in his hands. Why couldn't he save himself? I told his wife to bring him to the office in the morning.

At 6:00 a.m., we received a phone call that he was dead.

It is dangerous to put yourself in the place of the Almighty God. No one can exalt himself above the knowledge and power of God.

After the crusade, there was a great atmosphere of revival as everybody began to acknowledge the very existence of God and His power, an unusual thing in Flanders, Belgium. It was wonderful to witness the people opening their hearts to the Gospel.

Our ministry spread across the globe, on four continents - Africa, Europe, Asia, and America. The mission God gave me demonstrated the power to change lives through the Gospel of Jesus Christ. It was not just words, but also real action and influence for good all over the world.

As long as we focus on hope, anything is possible through belief in the power of God. As long as we are breathing with the breath of God, a great future lies before us. God has kept me alive to this day because He wants me to make a difference.

He wants you to make a difference, too. The world today desperately needs people who can make it a better place. You are here because of the mission you were born to fulfill. Maybe you do not even know it. It is time to find out why you are here. God, through his Son Jesus Christ, is ready to reveal it to you.

And whatever you do, remember one thing…

Jesus Christ is coming back very soon.

> *I am Alpha and Omega, the beginning and the ending, saith the Lord, which is, and which was, and which is to come, the Almighty (Revelation 1:8).*